Date: 2/12/21

BIO MARKOE
Markoe, Merrill,
We saw scenery : the early
diaries of Merrill Markoe /

WE SAW SCENERY

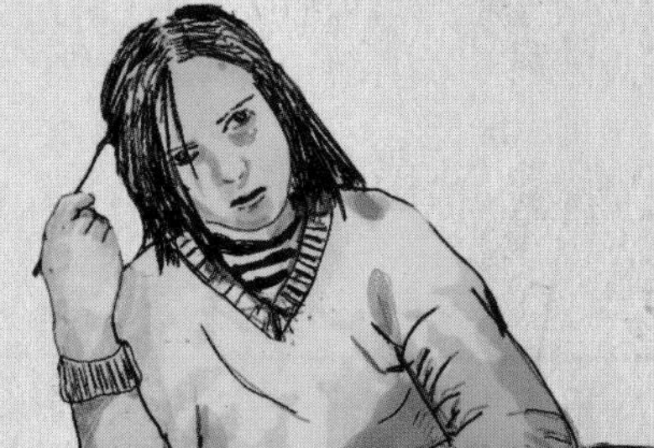

PALM BEACH COUNTY
LIBRARY SYSTEM
3650 SUMMIT BLVD.
WEST PALM BEACH, FL 33406

Also by Merrill Markoe

Late Night with David Letterman: The Book

How to Be Hap-Hap-Happy Like Me

Merrill Markoe's Guide to Love

*What the Dogs Have Taught Me:
And Other Amazing Things I've Learned*

It's My F---ing Birthday

The Psycho Ex Game

Walking in Circles Before Lying Down

Nose Down, Eyes Up

Cool, Calm, & Contentious

The Indignities of Being a Woman
(with Megan Koester)

MERRILL MARKOE

WE SAW SCENERY

THE EARLY DIARIES OF MERRILL MARKOE

ALGONQUIN BOOKS
OF CHAPEL HILL
2020

TUES. APRIL 7

I forgot
what
happened
today.

oh!
I went to school.
An thats it.

I also forgot
what happened
today.

hmm.
Oh yes, I went to
school. We worked.

That's right. How unusual!

Published by
Algonquin Books of Chapel Hill
Post Office Box 2225
Chapel Hill, North Carolina 27515-2225

a division of
Workman Publishing
225 Varick Street
New York, New York 10014

Printed in China.
Published simultaneously in Canada by Thomas Allen & Son Limited.
Design by Chad W. Beckerman.

Library of Congress Cataloging-in-Publication Data

Names: Markoe, Merrill, [date]– author.
Title: We saw scenery : the early diaries of Merrill Maroke / Merrill
   Markoe.
Description: Chapel Hill, North Carolina : Algonquin Books of Chapel Hill,
   [2020] | Summary: "A funny graphic memoir that takes us through the
   early diaries of Merrill Markoe (the original head writer for The
   David Letterman Show) and captures the difficulties of growing up
   and, ultimately, finding out that a smart mouth is a perfectly fine thing
   to have" — Provided by publisher.
Identifiers: LCCN 2020012681 | ISBN 9781616209032 (hardback) | ISBN
   9781643751177 (e-book)
Subjects: LCSH: Markoe, Merrill, [date]– —Comic books, strips, etc. |
   Television writers—United States—Biography—Comic books, strips, etc. |
Autobiographical comic books, strips, etc. | Graphic novels.
Classification: LCC PN1992.4.M35 A3 2020 | DDC 741.5/973—dc23
LC record available at https://lccn.loc.gov/2020012681

10 9 8 7 6 5 4 3 2 1
First Edition

CONTENTS

PART ONE : HEADED SOUTH

PART TWO : HEADED WEST

MON APRIL 27

I forgot
what happened
today.

PART ONE:
HEADED SOUTH

I KIND OF REMEMBER THAT ... I THINK

Let's start with a picture of me at home, where I live with four dogs.

There is also a human, a singer-songwriter, who has been in my life for 20 years . . . but he will not play a part in this particular story.

For the most part, it's a pretty standard domestic situation, except for the fact that in my mind I am Jane Goodall.

... even though for most of my life, I have worked as a humor writer. In the beginning, I wrote mainly for TV. My parents, who were alive then, were thrilled.

CONTENTS

PART ONE : HEADED SOUTH

PART TWO : HEADED WEST

I forgot
what happened
today.

PART ONE:
HEADED SOUTH

There are occupational hazards to being a writer. In addition to the emotional mess that can come from writing about the people you love, there is the physical mess that accumulates from seeing everything as a potential topic. Usually I save things that strike me as funny, thinking that maybe I'll write about them some day.

At least that is the excuse I give myself for the weird stuff in the boxes of things I don't get rid of because they make me laugh. . . .

FRESH HAIR!
Lush hair, custom molded so exactly, it bonds invisibly to your scalp.

Impossible to detect.

THE MOST natural hair replacement system ever! Come see for yourself!

HAIRART

1990-1991
Who's Who in the
Lunch Meat Industry

REJUVENATE WITH SACRED SEXUALITY
Sexual energy can be so powerful that it can heal sickness, diseases, and your emotions as well as create babies and help you manifest your desires.

There are also the many questionable mementos.
For instance, the MARKOE FOR TREASURER button
that I made in eighth grade ... the only real evidence
that my ill-fated run for a class office I never
really wanted actually happened.

It wasn't until the day that I decided to try and clean house that I found that little stack of childhood diaries I'd received as Christmas and birthday presents. They were lying way at the bottom of one of the biggest boxes.

Each one came with a lock and key, because
in the early sixties it was very important
for preteen girls in suburban housing
tracts to keep their dangerous secrets safe
from prying enemy eyes.

My
Diary
ONE YEAR DIARY BY HEART THROB ®

PROPERTY OF: Merrill, Markoe
80 N.E. 132 St.
Miami Fla.
11-8-1972

When I finally decided to sit down and read them, I was amazed at how much it felt like I was reading about a stranger.

Especially when I got to the eighth grade pages
and realized I'd kept a detailed record of everything that happened that time I ran for treasurer.

APRIL 13, 1963

Friday the thirteenth. What a day for a campaign speech.
Second period I fell down the stairs and ripped some
skin off my leg.

As anyone who knows an elderly person will tell you, the memories you have stored in your brain can be unreliable.

We are alive twenty-four hours a day, but only a tiny fraction of what we experience worms its way into the limbic system. That is where a part of the brain called the hippocampus turns some short-term memories into long-term memories.

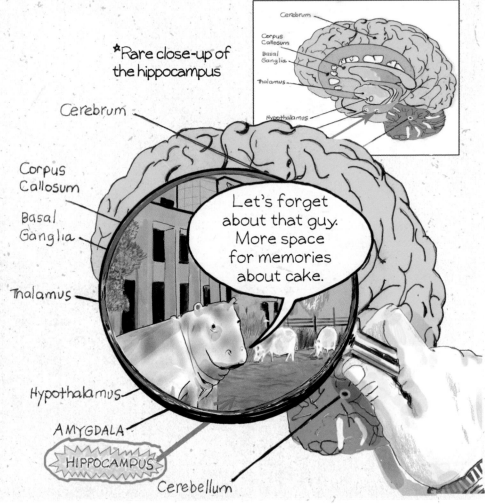

*Rare close-up of the hippocampus

Cerebrum

Corpus Callosum

Basal Ganglia

Thalamus

Hypothalamus

AMYGDALA

HIPPOCAMPUS

Cerebellum

Let's forget about that guy. More space for memories about cake.

But even after a memory has been granted tenure in the hippocampus, the landscape of the place still feels like this.

On the other hand, if you happen to have everything
written down, as I did, you at least wind up with
a few detailed, if age-locked, accounts of what happened.

MARCH 16, 1960

Today I was almost the winner of the sixth grade spelling
bee. I ended up as the runner-up. I missed a stupid word
I knew because I was nervous. Nancy Larson won.

That doesn't mean they contain any perspective.

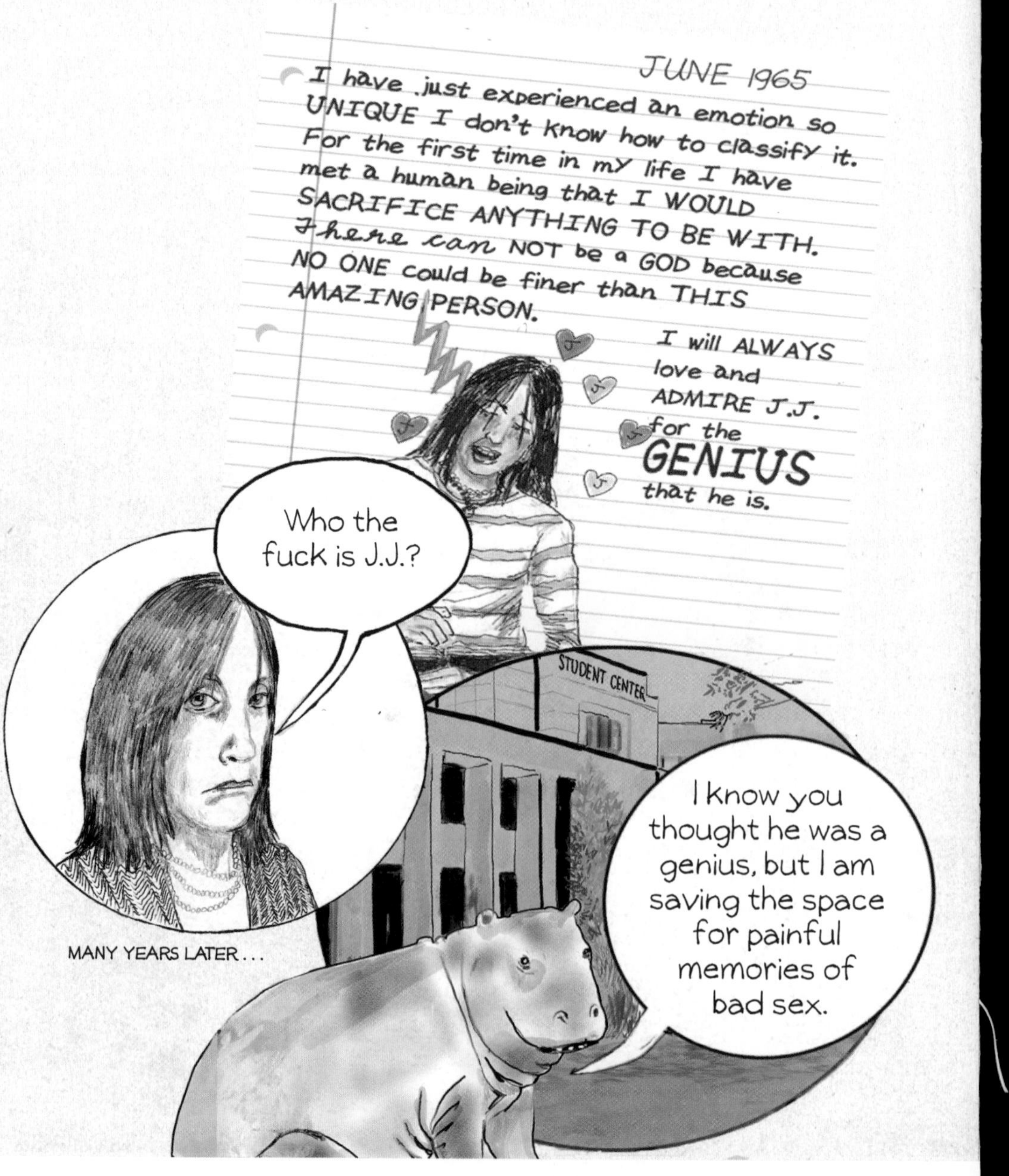

1: NORTH MIAMI

When I began writing the first diary it was 1958. The family business, which my dad took over from his dad, had just gone bankrupt. He decided to move us from New Jersey to North Miami, Florida.

So there he was, the father of two small children, facing a very unsettling event. It was one that I never heard him mention.

There were some visual clues. But I was too young to understand them.

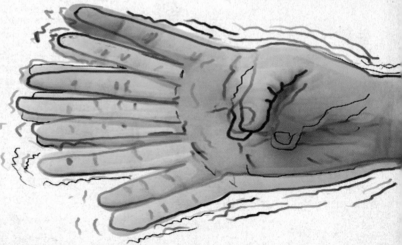

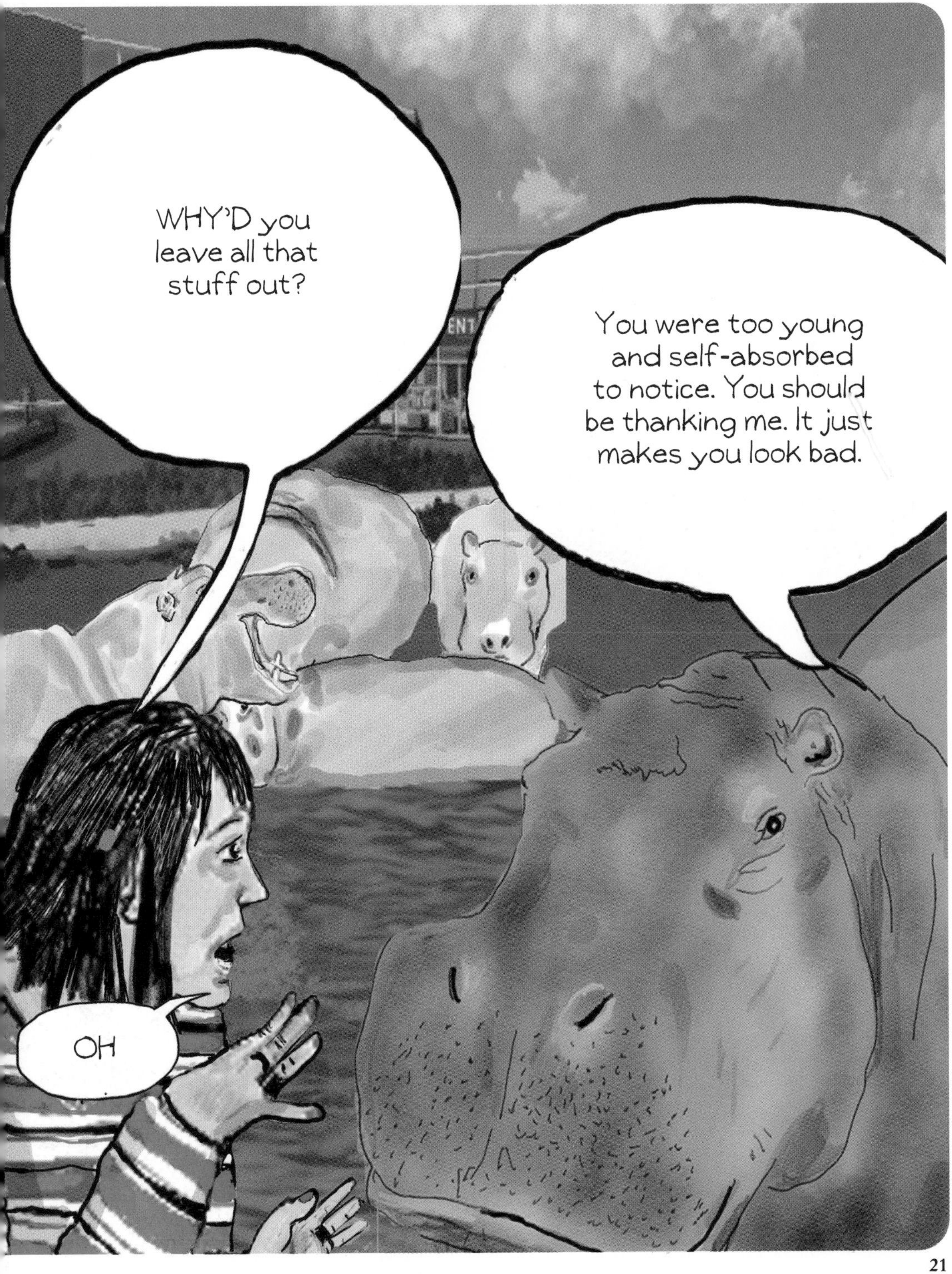
WHY'D you leave all that stuff out?
You were too young and self-absorbed to notice. You should be thanking me. It just makes you look bad.
OH

Here's how it landed in the hippocampus: One minute I was rehearsing for a Christmas pageant as one of several children who had to sit absolutely still on a sled in an attempt to recreate a Norman Rockwell painting.

After that, cut to a few black-and-white establishing shots of a motel room somewhere in Miami where my mother is trying to open a coconut she found lying on the ground by hurling it onto the floor.

Though the more I think about this scene, the more I see it in color.

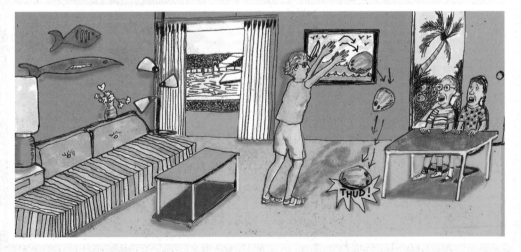

Florida seemed haunted. It was full
of incongruous and unsettling images
coexisting side by side.

Disgusted by the all-too-common symbols of racism and stupidity we encountered, my mother would try to make fun of them.

But every time we drove past the Kenilworth Hotel on our way to the beach, my mother would mention how, in the fifties, it was partially owned by television personality Arthur Godfrey, who recorded his show in the penthouse.

PENTHOUSE

Then she would add that she'd heard that there was a sign in the lobby that said "No Jews or dogs allowed."

It made me feel sick to my stomach.

One more reason I was pleased and relieved that I found the Arthur Godfrey show completely unwatchable.

2: EARLY DNA

So anyway, when I sat down to read these
diaries, I was wondering if the original-recipe
version of me in grade school would remind me
of the geezer version of me who had become a writer.

*Not a likeness of
the author

Was I always her? Or were there points along the way where another outcome was possible?

Would that
transformation
be visible on
these pages?

TWENTY-ONE DAYS !
I'm SO OLD. And FAT.
My cocoon barely fits
anymore.

They say the opening line of a book is a good indication of what is to come.

January 1, 1959
Dear Diary,
Today the weather was not too nice. Little Bruce came over. Today Bruce got bitten by a slug. I used my new roller skates. That was fun.

Well, I was certainly NO Anne Frank.

To be fair, at ten years of age I had only been on this planet for about 3,650 days, which is a pretty short period of time. Unless you're a squirrel, in which case it is your entire life span.

yesterday we saw an ice berg. It looked like a great ice mountain We went down into the second and third class but found we could not go into the engine room. The had a field day but I wa... and didnt go I... I felt better ...y they had a ...t to that ...board on

Of course statistics like these are so relative. At the age of ten, Ernest Hemingway made his first attempt at writing fiction in his diary. Now fans and critics gleefully scour it as a way to further scrutinize his work.

My early work took a slightly less complicated tack. My philosophy appears to have been "TRY TO WRITE SOMETHING ON EVERY PAGE."

APRIL 13, 1959

Today in school we had a substitute teacher named Mrs. Kadish. She did everything backwards.

It was interesting to see which moments had made it into the hippocampus. A lot of what I found on these pages the adult me had forgotten. For instance, I remembered this attempt at creative cooking.

SATURDAY, JANUARY 21, 1961

I cooked dinner for the family tonight. I made something like a hamburger only it was on a popsicle stick. Also carrots.

But a day labeled "One of the worst days I have ever known" had dissolved completely into the cloudy soup of time.

TUESDAY, JUNE 7, 1960

Today was one of the worst days I have ever known. First Mr. Wilson yapped at me all day in school. And then at piano lessons, Miss Clemson started yapping at me that if I didn't stay alert I could go find another teacher. So I quit.

I feel lower than I have ever felt before.

I had even forgotten this critical moment, which, in restrospect, was important enough to have undermined my self-image and sent me spiraling into a lifetime of obsessive dieting.

TUESDAY, JUNE 14, 1960

I had to go to the dumb old doctor for a checkup and he told me I have to LOSE WEIGHT. Then STUPID IDIOTIC Glenn started teasing me and calling me fat. So I hit him. This resulted in a big fight and Mom took sides with bum-headed Glenn! He blamed it on me, and now I have to get PUNISHED for it.

Time for a diet young lady

One careless quip from some unremembered
doctor and my life was changed forever.
Yet I had blanked it out.

It was fun to get reacquainted with words
I wouldn't recall even under sodium pentothal.

But it was only after diary prompting that I was able to recall the details of family trips to Florida's top vacation spots where we saw something I referred to as scenery. Apparently the hippocampus didn't care much for scenery.

NOVEMBER 4, 1960 FAMILY TRIP

NO school because it is Thanksgiving. We decided to go to the Everglades. It took about 3 hours. We got a nice room and had Thanksgiving dinner there and also went on a boat ride.

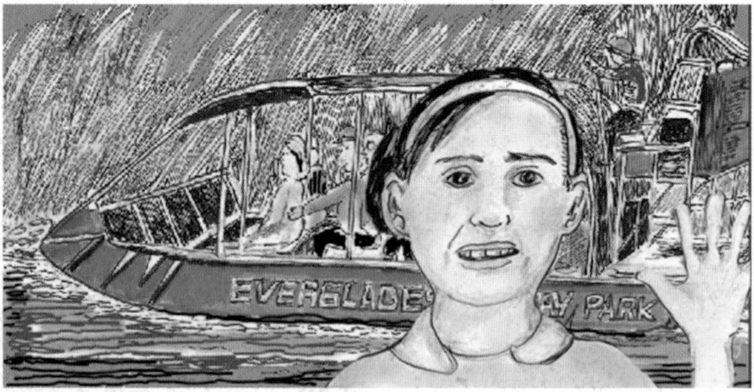
EVERGLADES
PARK

We saw scenery.

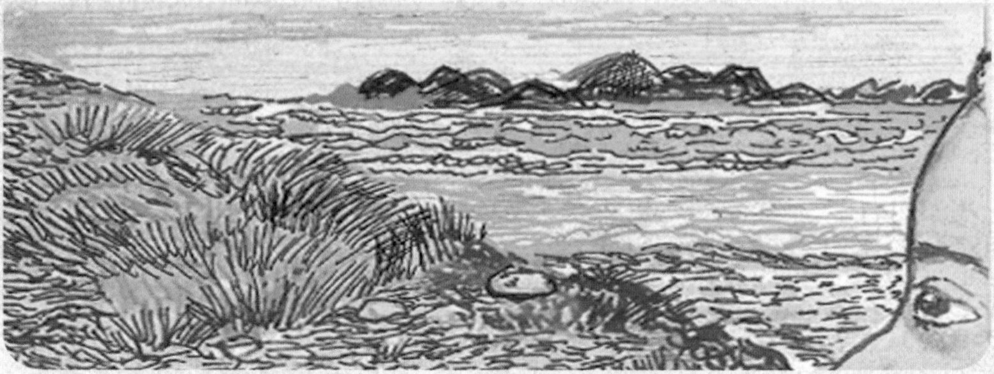

It appears that the hippocampus favored feelings of disgust over feelings of benign boredom, because I can still remember that disappointing sandwich but that "nice" theater of the sea has disappeared entirely.

NOVEMBER 26, 1960 FAMILY TRIP, CONT.

Today we skipped school and started for the Florida Keys. The weather was clear and cold. We ate lunch at a TERRIBLE place along the way. It couldn't possibly be worse.

We stopped at the Theater of the Sea. It was nice.

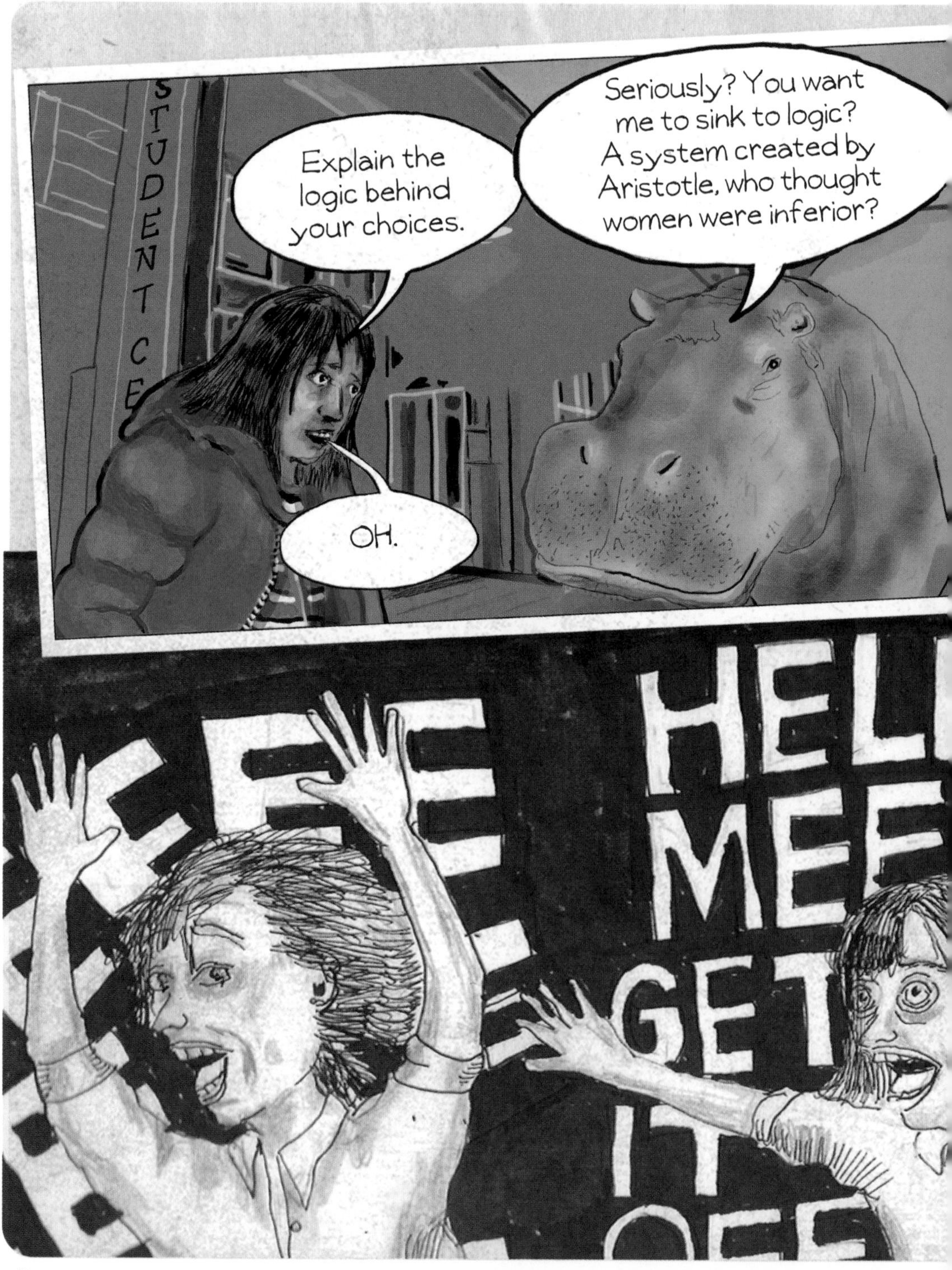
STUDENT CE
Explain the logic behind your choices.
Seriously? You want me to sink to logic? A system created by Aristotle, who thought women were inferior?
OH.
HEL
MEE
GET
IT

Naturally I remembered this frightening incident, which later made us laugh so hard, we both overlooked the fact that I had run screaming from my friend who needed help.

APRIL 8, 1962

Andi came over. When she walked in, she had a big palmetto bug on her back! She ran after me screaming, "Get it off me," but I screamed and ran away. I was so loud that Glenn came running out of the shower stark nude. We finally got it off her.

PALMETTO BUG
(Eurycotis floridiana)

I definitely remembered the Jilmer Club . . .
the only club named for me (and my friend Jill).
Partly because we held meetings for a year.

FRIDAY JANUARY 15, 1959

Jill and I had a Jilmer meeting. We rented the boys' club house for 5 cents a half hour, but then we refused to pay them because there were too many flies.

But mainly because the hippocampus seems to have endorsed memories that involved laughter. The entire club membership was willfully silly.

JANUARY 20, 1960

At our Jilmer meeting, we went to the beach. We had a good time spying on people.

TUESDAY, JUNE 7, 1960

The only good time I had today was that Jill and I called in a dedication on the radio. We said, "FOR THE JILMER CLUB," and the disc jockey said:

THAT was soOOO funny!

Am I right? Are you guys prioritizing admissions for funny stuff?
Well, we do enjoy a good laugh. But we save A LOT of space for HIDEOUS stuff as well.
I'm curious. What's a popular joke on the hippocampus this semester?
Mostly puns about the length of the short grasses everyone is eating. You heard this one?
Oh. Mmm hmm. Maybe you had to be there.
STUD

I was also surprised by this: On the last page of my first diary, written on a blank page meant to contain some kind of a Christmas list, was this pompous little message to an imaginary readership. It was the first sign that I was writing for an audience.

Christmas List

I think if many of the parents today who are raising children had saved their old diaries it would be easier to help their kids through adolesence

Why did the kid version of me feel the need to insert such a piece of self-serving bullshit into this otherwise unpretentious document?

Dear Diary...
I'm writing in the hopes that when people of the future read about my fights with my brother, it will heal the world and bring peace.

My friends and I weren't exactly in the universal truths business. So who was I addressing? Who was I trying to impress?

3: PRIME DEMOGRAPHIC

It was at this point that I realized I didn't understand my younger self too well. There were questions about the life we shared that I couldn't answer.

Sometimes she seemed like that replicant version of my mother that I have spent my entire life trying not to become.

MAY 20, 1960

Today was our sixth grade party. It wasn't much fun. I was rather disappointed. They served these INEDIBLE hot dogs. THE WORST. I ate with Jill and some kids from her class. They were really noisy.

BAD FOOD. Horrible ambiance. EVERYTHING subpar.

One thing was very clear. In my new home in North Miami, I'd turned into one of those annoying preteen kids so steeped in pop culture that I called up every radio station that asked for callers, joined all the clubs on the backs of cereal boxes, and entered every contest advertised on TV. Unsurprisingly, the card I played involved trying to be funny.

DECEMBER 15, 1958
TODAY I GOT GLASSES.
Also today on *The Jim Dooley Show*, Jim Dooley read my letter during the Mr. Moke contest about why you would like Mr. Moke to come to your party. HE READ IT ON TV!!

I bet Mr. Moke would be more fun than most of my friends.

Just because they read it on TV doesn't mean YOU WON ANYTHING!

Oh MY GOD. MOM! SOMEONE!!!

Mr Moke

In this manner did I score a lot of free T-shirts and promotional items.

MAY 1, 1959 FRIDAY

Today I received a letter saying I won a T-shirt from the Sessions School Day Peanut Butter "Name the Peanut" contest. I entered five times but they didn't say which name I entered won. I also received a recording of "The Sessions School Day Peanut Butter Song": the exact same one they use on the commercial on television!!!

My new obsessions led to multiple encounters with the local celebrities who hosted the kids shows I still watched.

FEBRUARY 28, 1959

After piano lessons, we went to Grand Union where Jim Dooley came in a helicopter with Mr. Moke and they handed out Jim Dooley potato chips. I got his autograph. He looks MUCH older in person.

Within this modestly talented group of men, my favorite was M.T. Graves of *The Dungeon* ... an almost funny Saturday night show that played theoretically scary movies. So when a friend of my parents offered me a chance to ride with him in a limo to the opening of a shopping center, I was really thrilled. At last, a chance to interrogate him mercilessly.

So imagine my excitement a few months later when I saw him again. I couldn't tell if he recognized me, but if he did, he was definitely less excited about our reunion than I was.

MARCH 18, 1960

Tonight we went to a ballet to see *Swan Lake* and we saw M.T. Graves (alias Charlie Baxter) from *The Dungeon*. He was sitting a few rows in front of us in the audience and he really looked different without makeup. I asked him to sign my program and he did.

By now, pop culture had become the glue that held my life together.

JULY 16, 1960

Today Kathy, Glenn, Norman, and I went to Loew's 170th St. Theatre to see *The Bellboy* starring Jerry Lewis. It was GREAT! After on WCKR radio station they have this contest where you call and sing and they record it and every once in a while they play back five voices and if you are the first to call and identify your voice, you win TEN DOLLARS!!!

Happy WCKR

Happy WCKR

My life revolved around the TV and radio schedules
I had memorized. As with any intense relationship,
there were highs . . .

SATURDAY, JULY 9, 1960

At night I was sitting in my room listening to the radio and
playing that game Bonejammer. Whenever the DJ yells
it, if you call them and get through first they send you a
free record.

And there were lows.

OCTOBER 11, 1960

The TV doesn't work so I am suffering with the agony of MISSING MY SHOWS!!!

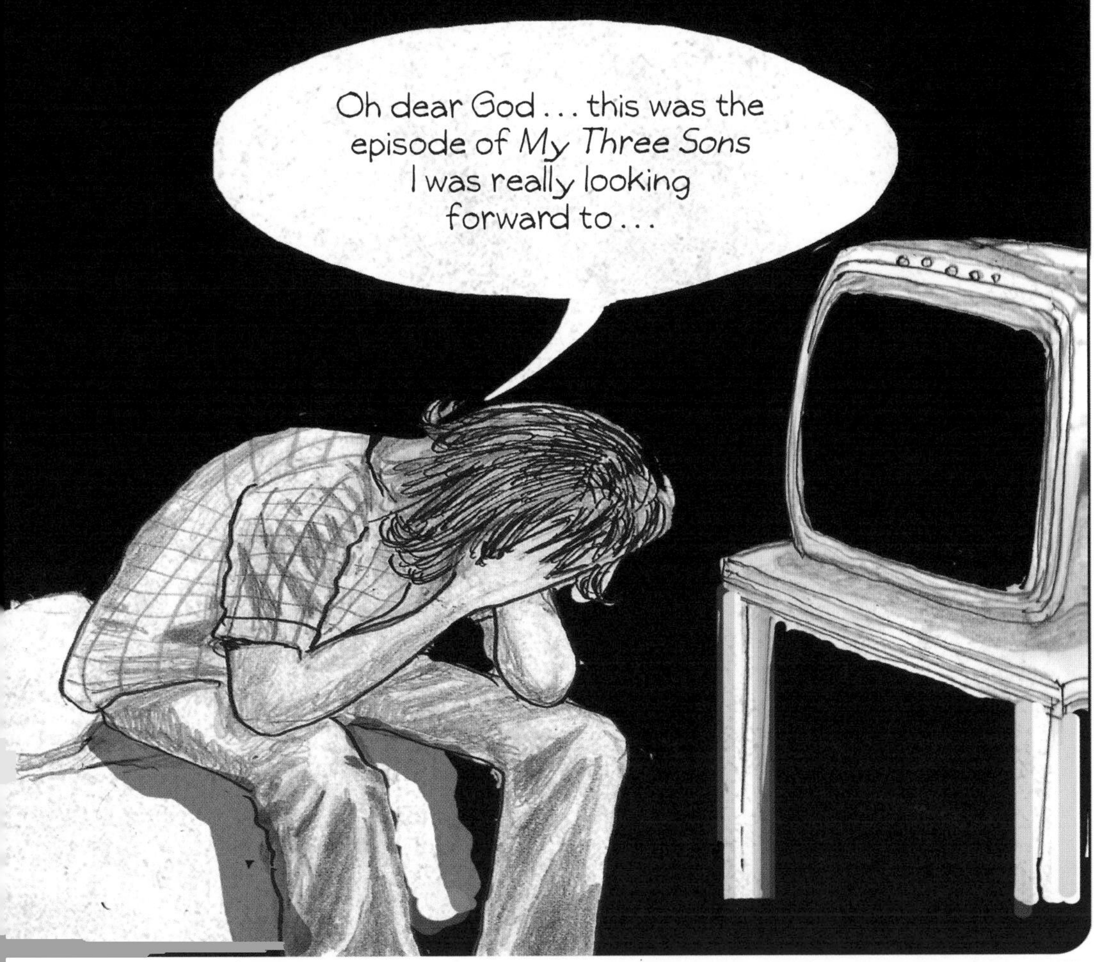
Oh dear God . . . this was the episode of *My Three Sons* I was really looking forward to . . .

The best part of every day for me was always 3:30 . . . because after school I could reenter the world of everything I valued. I was an ideal audience member: accepting and nonjudgmental. Prime demographic.

JANUARY 8, 1960

At night I watched *Cheyenne* and KOOKIE was on it. He played a bad guy and at the end he got hanged. It was so sad, I started to cry.

TV was my best friend. Although from time to time, we had our disagreements.

JULY 13, 1960

In the evening they ran the Democratic Convention on TV for the third day! They nominated some guy for president. The one with the best chance is JOHN (JACK) KENNEDY.

It was TV that saved me from social oblivion by showing me how to redirect my bottomless yearning.

SEPTEMBER 18, 1960

Today I watched the greatest show I ever saw. It was called *National Velvet* and it's about a horse. My lifelong desire to own a horse just doubled. Now I want one so bad I am going to save until I get one. I know one day soon I will get a horse.

I need to live in a show like this.

From that point on, as long as I could get a ride
to the stables, I could enter an arena where
I was living in my own show.

DECEMBER. 10-17
Rode Mousie.
Did cantering.

DECEMBER 24-31
Rode Honeycomb.

NOVEMBER 19-2
Rode Giddy.
Brought a
whole bag
of carrots.

FEBRUARY 28, 1962

In the morning, I rode Dark Rhythm. Everyone else I know hates him. But he's real gentle around me and he rubs his head on my arm. It's kind of like a story in a book or a movie. We were made for each other. (Choke. Sob.)

At night I rode Blaze in a show. We trotted on the right diagonal and cantered on the left lead. And I won first place.
A blue ribbon! Me!
AMAZING!

4: THE ANTAGONIST

Every historical saga has a relentless adversary.
At this point, it was my brother.

JANUARY 29, 1959

Today I am mad at Glenn. He is a very greedy boy. When it was MY birthday party, I had to let him eat with the girls and play all the games. But now that it is HIS party, he said I had to eat at a separate table from them and couldn't even go on the rides. But I still went on Crazy Castle and Boats, Trains, and Planes!

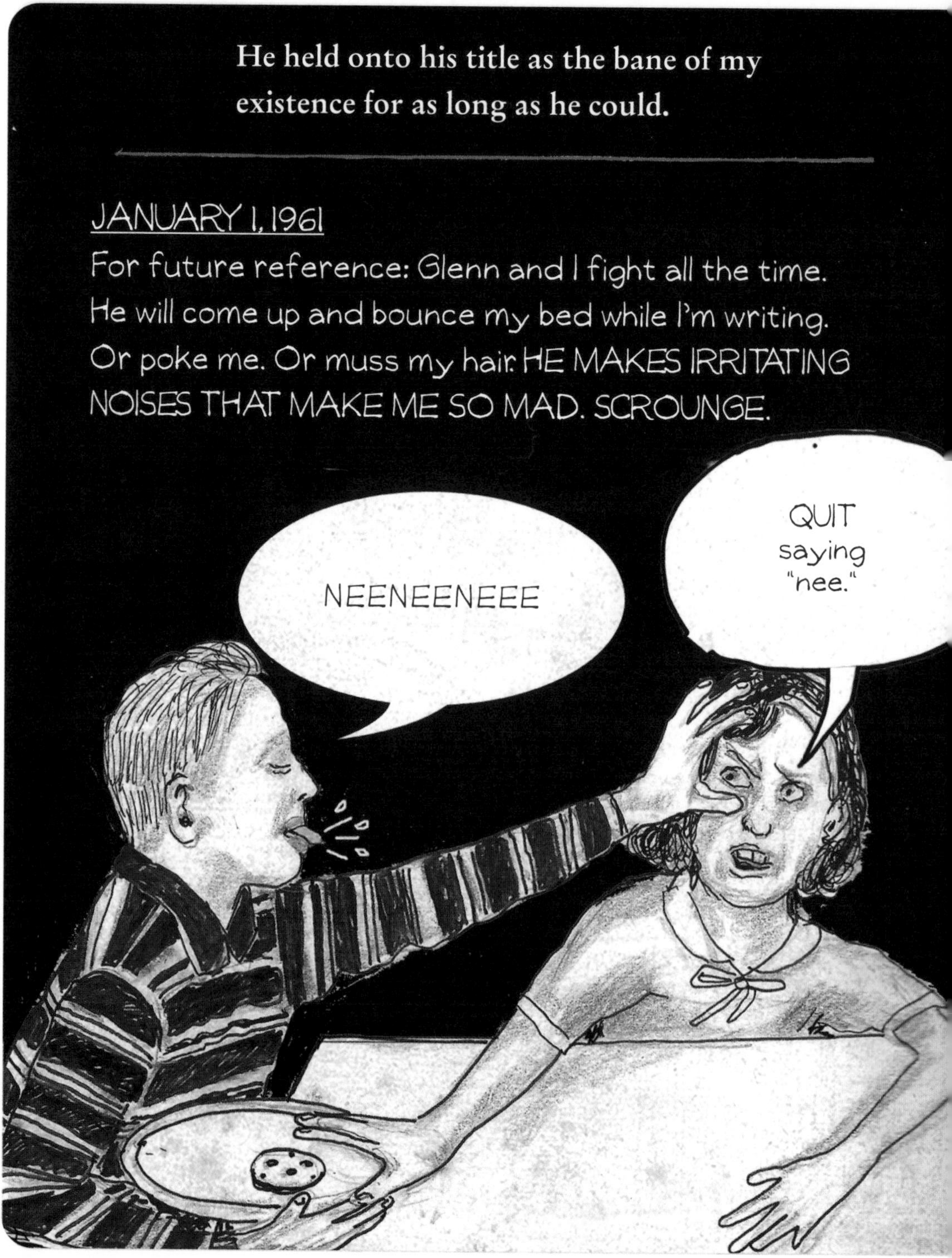
He held onto his title as the bane of my existence for as long as he could.
JANUARY 1, 1961
For future reference: Glenn and I fight all the time. He will come up and bounce my bed while I'm writing. Or poke me. Or muss my hair. HE MAKES IRRITATING NOISES THAT MAKE ME SO MAD. SCROUNGE.
NEENEENEEE
QUIT saying "nee."

MARCH 3, 1961
GLENN IS AN
IDIOT and I can
not live a good life
without him teasing
me every minute
of the day …

Twenty-five years later he would become this lovely guy known as Dr. Markoe, who wrote a book on the Phoenicians and lectured on topics like "the funerary iconography of the lotus flower."

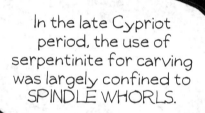

I guess he had to develop other interests when his role was usurped by a much stronger force field: my very angry mother. She was far better equipped to deliver on her threats.

MONDAY, APRIL 18, 1960

Tonight I started watching a real good show. It was only 9:30 and Mom came in and turned it off right in the middle of the show. I called her "a big meanie" and all of a sudden she started yelling at me again. She seems to be ALWAYS yelling at me. Anything I do, I get YELLED AT. Sometimes even when I am GOOD, I get yelled at.

TURN THIS BLASTED THING OFF.

Why?

Because I said so, that's why. I am NOT your friend. I am YOUR MOTHER.

5: SCOUTS

In my first diary, I was preparing for a "Fly-Up." It was symbolism-filled ceremony where a Brownie crosses a special bridge, takes a pledge, and and magically becomes a Girl Scout. Unfortunately the seeds of who I was to become had already taken root. It was too late to keep me from finding the whole thing funny.

JANUARY 29, 1959

Then this evening our Brownie troop had a Girl Scout Fly-Up. I goofed up the whole show by giggling.

Oh my God. That BRIDGE.

No wonder that was the last paramilitary pastry sales force I ever joined.

Nevertheless, the very next day I browbeat my mother into taking me to the Girl Scout–approved outlet store so I could replace my lackluster Brownie uniform with an even more unflattering green one.

JANUARY 30, 1959

Today we went to Richard's to get my Girl Scout uniform. We got the hat, the socks, the wallet, the emblem, and the belt. We had hot dogs for lunch at Corky's Restaurant. They were a mile long. At least that's what they claim.

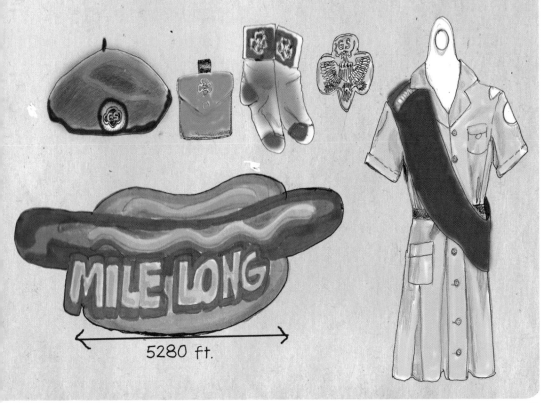

MILE LONG

5280 ft.

After all that symbolic buildup, I was expecting the new, more mature incarnation of our troop to zero in on the adventure and excitement implicit in the word *Scout*.

I was deeply disappointed when, instead, our troop began doubling down on the word *girl*.

THURSDAY, MARCH 29

Today was Girl Scouts and our troop saw a movie called *The Story of Menstruation*. It was interesting. I had five glasses of lemonade.

Perhaps that explains why the content of these meetings didn't make it into the hippocampus. I only remembered them because I read about them. Even Juliette Low, creator of the Girl Scouts, might have been surprised at how far from the idea of scouting our troop had begun to drift.

OCTOBER 8, 1959

Today at Girl Scouts we had a cooking lesson at the gas store on 125th street.

Behold the mighty tablespoon, ladies.

We cut out pictures and recipes for our cooking notebook. Then we discussed cooking measures and terms.

Our leaders, my mom included, seemed to see scouting as a school for future housewives.

JANUARY 28, 1960
Today in Girl Scouts, Miss Meat showed us how to cook three kinds of eggs; poached, fried, and baked.

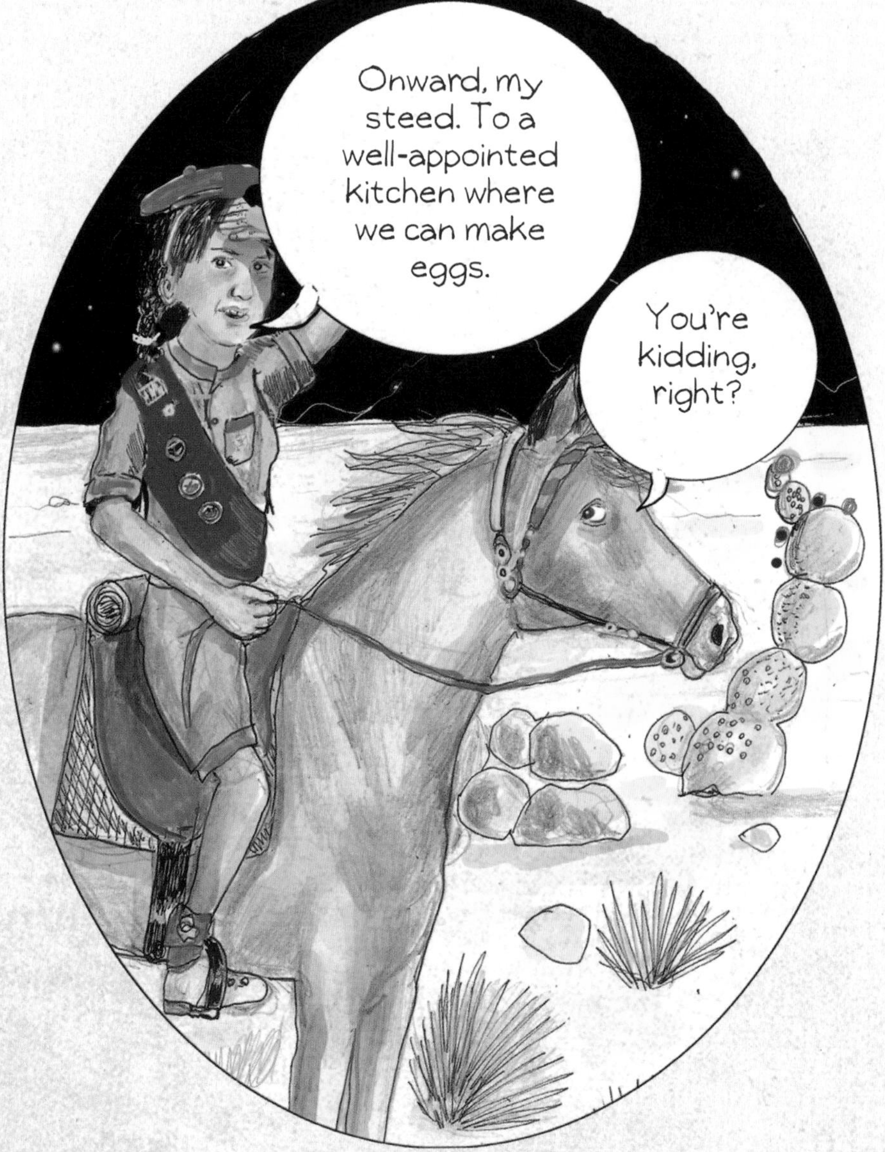
Onward, my steed. To a well-appointed kitchen where we can make eggs.
You're kidding, right?

There were other reasons I got fed up with scouting.

THURSDAY, JANUARY 21, 1960

Today in Girl Scouts we had to practice and practice and practice "Dance with Us, Sing with Us, Gretchen and Hans." It's a babyish little Dutch song that Linda found in a first grade piano book, where you march around in a circle stamping your feet while you sing it. We had to practice it over and over because it's SO HARD TO LEARN (haha). I am going to be so ashamed on Juliette Low Day.

I was developing what my mother and my grand-mother called "an ATTITUDE."

Inside of that attitude was an X-ray of me turning into myself.

MARCH 11, 1960

Today our troop leader called Mom and said she didn't think Jill and I liked her anymore because we were always talking to each other during meetings. Then Mom yelled at me and said I can't talk in Girl Scouts anymore.

I washed my hair.

6: LOVE

The truth was that, on the pages of these diaries, thanks to my good friend TV, I was preparing myself for the more exciting and dangerous life I was destined to live as a teen.

MARCH 29, 1959

Today I decided that I would NOT wear any lipstick or makeup until I am in my twenties. In fact, I might NEVER. WEAR IT.

NOVEMBER 10, 1959

Today I decided that I was NOT going to wait until I am 18 to wear lipstick but might wear it when I am 14.

Acting like a child seemed a waste of my valuable time because ever since fourth grade I had been "in a relationship." Okay, yes, maybe I was having this "relationship" by myself, but this was definitely not the last time this would happen.

MARCH 29, 1959
MY BOYFRIEND IS WAYNE WALKER.
He is VERY CUTE. I like him VERY MUCH
(SOMETIMES!) Sometimes I hate him!!!

Little girls tend to be delusional about love. But I managed to lower the bar substantially by finding a way to interpret the German salute my one true love gave me as some sort of coded flirtation.

JANUARY 14, 1959

Today in school we went to see a movie with Szita's class. But as soon as I entered the room WAYNE stood UP and said out loud in front of everyone "ACH TOONG" and then went like this. The NERVE!

I believed there was evidence that our love was heating up because I was getting all my romantic advice from *Mad* magazine. This was the first but not the last time I would learn sarcasm was not a good tool for seduction.

MAY 26, 1959

TODAY was the last Girl Scout meeting. (HOORAY!)
I drew a picture on a piece of paper and I wrote:

To WAYNE

Roses are red
VIOLETS are blue
I KILLED MY DOG
cause he looked like YOU.

Then Jill and I left it on his bike. I wonder if he found it.

The only Jewish kid dumb enough to confuse a Nazi salute with a flirtation. On the bright side,

no need to waste time wondering what HE is up to these days.

JUNE 2, 1960

I decided I LOVE Wayne more than ANY of the others. When I went in to his class, HE STOOD UP IN FRONT OF EVERYONE AND SAID:

These pages were so painful to read that I had no choice but to sit my younger self down and have a frank talk with her. Was she stupid? Or was Wayne breaking new ground as the world's most ironic flirt?

To be fair, in rereading other passages in the diary that described how the boys of this age treated the girls, it wasn't impossible to see how I could have made this insane mistake.

Thursday
JANUARY 7 1960

After school we had Girl Scouts. Just a little before that Wayne started teasing Kathy and me. I was holding everyone's books. He gave me a pat on the back and everything dropped.

So you had no idea what a Nazi salute meant?

He was paying attention to me because he LIKES me.

You don't understand anything!

In school at lunch it was really funny. Wayne was teasing me. I waved at Jill and he waved at me. Then Jill told me to sleep over her house and Wayne said

He is such a doll.

In my mind, Wayne and I were costarring in one of those temporarily fraught romances from one of those sixties movies that I loved: tales of mismatched couples who didn't get along at first. The men, who dressed in suits, made contact with the gals by offering sidelong glances. The women, in sleeveless sheath dresses, found themselves at wit's end trying to cope with these seemingly impossible fellas. But in the end, the women would win this "battle of the sexes" by making the men believe it had been their idea in the first place. Next thing you know, a wedding would be planned!

It always worked out for Rock Hudson and Doris Day when they least expected it. There was no reason to believe it wouldn't work out for me and Wayne. How could it not? And so the fires of my love continued to burn.

Not only did I not see his Jew-baiting as an obstacle, I saw encouraging signs of progress everywhere! Exhibit A: Jackie's party, where he almost asked me to dance. That dangling and possibly imaginary "almost" meant everything.

SATURDAY, APRIL 2, 1960

Today was Jackie's party. It was fun. A lot of boys stuck their shoes in the pool.

I almost danced with Wayne. He was only a few feet away, coming toward me, when a nutty girl grabbed me.

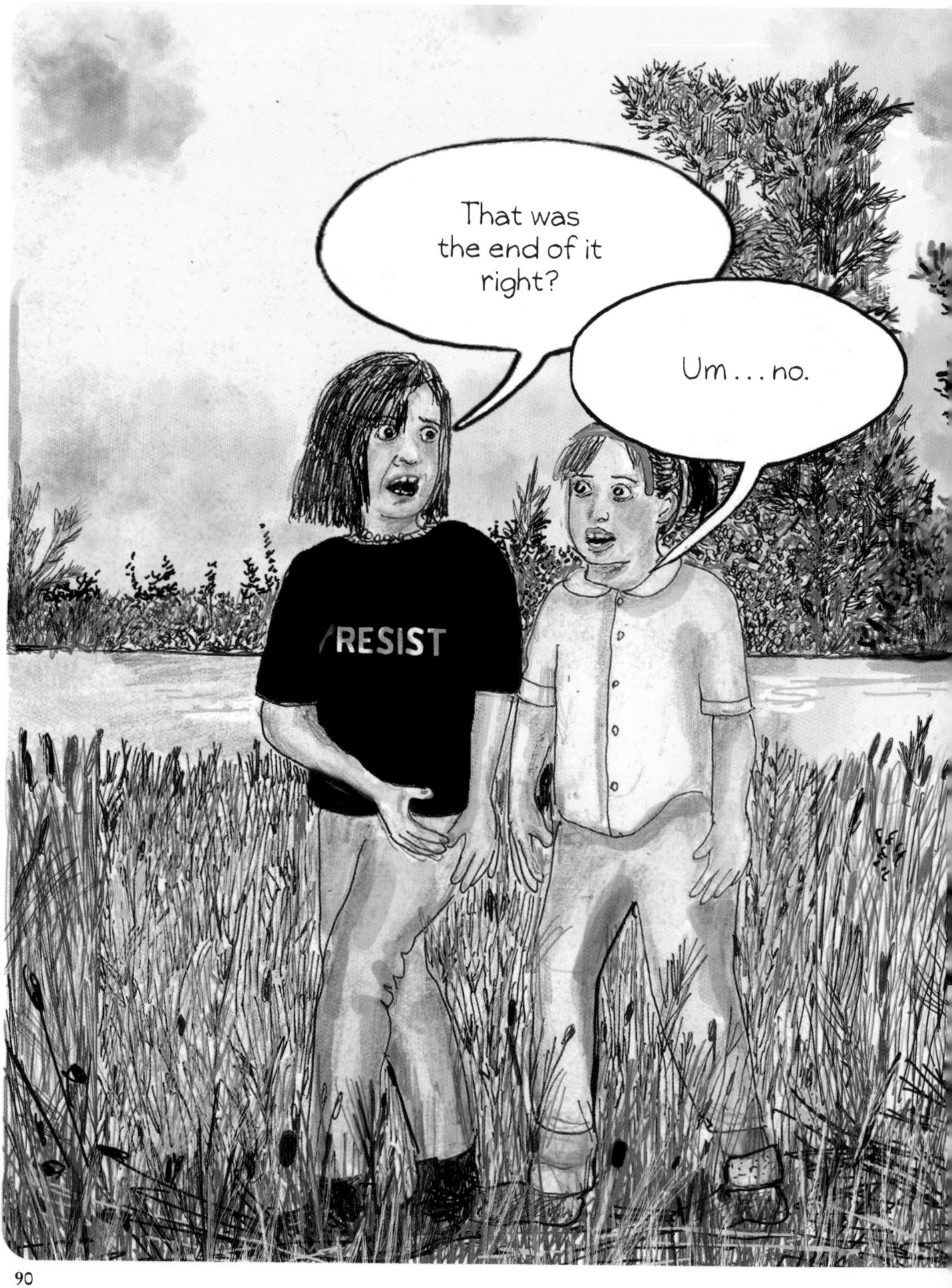

That was the end of it right?
Um . . . no.
RESIST

The highlight of this very special relationship was still to come when I had a once-in-a-lifetime chance to experience the minimum definition of "a dream."

FRIDAY, MAY 6, 1960

TODAY when I was waiting for Jill after school, I screwed up my courage and asked Wayne to sign my autograph book. He said "Okay, just a minute." Then guess what? I got it. He wrote:

> To a nice girl and luck in seventh grade. Wayne

WHAT A DREAM! I LOVE him so much!!

I reread that blessed autograph all summer.
It seemed filled with hidden meanings, none of which
were remotely connected to the Third Reich.

7: THE TREACHERY OF JUNIOR HIGH

Junior High seems like it was much more nerve-wracking than this "middle school" everyone attends now. Almost everything about it could be placed under the dual headings of both Pretentious and Intimidating.

SERIOUSLY! "THEE" ?????

Alma Mater, Alma Mater
North Miami Junior High.
Let the world know that we love thee
North Miami Junior High.

The structure that housed North Miami Junior High was originally a tiger zoo used by the Clyde Beatty Circus. How I wish I could have attended while the tigers were still in residence.

Absent the comforting distraction of vicious wild felines, I began every day with a stomachache.

SEPTEMBER 6, 1960
Today I went to Jr. High and I did not like it very much. The food is horrible and so are the teachers.

Ew. Disgusting.

This was the year of the first big Cuban immigration to Miami, which meant that a lot of attractive and intimidating Cuban boys enrolled. Unfortunately, they turned out to be just another tier of cute guys who wanted nothing to do with me.

As it turned out, Girl Scouts wasn't the only venue that was pushing housewifery. I had to take Home Ec . . . a girls-only requirement where the classroom was basically a kitchen. Our opening assignment was to make a fruit salad by opening a can of fruit cocktail.

I was shockingly terrible at sewing.

MARCH 4, 1961

In Home Ec we started a new unit, which is SEWING. We are going to make GATHERED SKIRTS. I can already tell that mine is going to look like a brightly colored spitball. ALSO, for additional fun, we have to memorize all the parts of the sewing machine. Who the hell knows why she thinks we have to do that.

For some reason I was placed into "accelerated math," a subject for which I felt I had no aptitude. Luckily a lack of interest in math was something the teacher and I had in common.

FEBRUARY 4, 1961

In accelerated math, Mr. Draper showed us MORE slides. This time of his trip around the United States. He had some beautiful slides, but let's face it: looking at slides is NOT VERY INTERESTING!

> You kids will get a kick out of this. My son Steve by the Grand Canyon when he was your age. NOW he's THIRTY-SEVEN!

Minna and I were literally COUNTING THE MINUTES until the bell.

Then there was the joy of phys ed. the year President Kennedy ordered mandatory physical education fitness training to help our nation's flabby youth become more competitive with the Russians.

FEBRUARY 13, 1961

Phys Ed. Today was a thrill a minute. First we had PULL UPS. 40 was an A. I could only do ONE. Then we had SOFTBALL THROW and I only threw it 48 feet. 50 was passing. One girl threw it 138 feet. I guess I am not the world's greatest athlete. I'M THE SECOND GREATEST.

We also had to take ballroom dancing for a month. Maybe the Russians were ahead of us there, too.

FEBRUARY 15, 1961

In Phys Ed. we started dancing. The one I danced with was knee high to a grasshopper. I always get the short ones.

No, that's your big mistake. It's one-two-three, one-two-three.

Only 5 minutes to the bell . . .

One and uh two and uh

The requirements for teaching at NMJHS must have been pretty low key. My seventh grade English teacher, Mrs. Derrington, shaved her legs and tweezed her eyebrows during a spelling test.

I wish I could report that I had given up on human boys. But when my Nazi boyfriend was assigned to a different school, he was quickly replaced by Bobby, another boy who fit my meticulous relationship requirements of showing no particular interest.

FEBRUARY 13, 1961
I LOVE BOBBY.

He is: darling, adorable, sweet, cute, handsome, lovable, great, attractive, terrific, stupendous, marvelous. He has a good personality and is a good dancer. I love him.

I judged the relationship to be a success on the basis of another end-of-the-year signature in my autograph book . . . more of the naïve optimism about the opposite sex that would plague me for the entire rest of my life.

JUNE 6, 1961 THE LAST DAY OF SCHOOL, GRADE SEVEN.

In English, stupid old Mrs. Derrington asked us who had *World Books* and who didn't, because she sells them in the summer. I asked Bobby if he had signed my autograph book yet.

He started looking through all his books for it. I didn't think he'd find it, but he did. He wrote:

Roses are red Violets are blue
Sugar is sweet and so is you
Good luck with all your
boyfriends next year.

Here, um. OKAY. Well, have a NICE VACATION.

I love him. When the bell ran, I waved goodbye. I'm sure he likes me now.

103

Over the summer I spent a couple of weeks at a camp, where I appear to have taken a turn toward the introspective . . .

SUNDAY, JULY 9, 1961
I LOVE BOBBY.
Today I got up the courage to go off the high diving board. When you jump off it, you get the queerest sensation when you feel yourself falling like a piece of lead through the air. Suddenly I realize that summer is going by awful quickly. I don't want school to start.

Whee. Look at me! Definitely NOT thinking about Bobby.

Camp was mostly uneventful, except when I was able to apply my growing smartass skills to undermining classic songs from beloved Broadway musicals. It was a relief to find a camp activity at which I could excel.

JULY 29, 1961 CAMP LEAR

Today in camp we presented *South Pacific*, which we rehearsed for 2 long weeks. I had a few parts. I sang along with Kathy in "Wash That Man." But my favorite was when three boys sang "There Is Nothing Like a Dame." Then Kathy and I walk in looking like slobs.

8: THE INSURMOUNTABLE OBSTACLES OF EIGHTH GRADE

It seemed like everything in my life had just been but a rehearsal for this year, where the goal was to achieve a level of cuteness that was beyond reproach. This was the year I discovered that I was cuteness-challenged.

OCTOBER 1, 1961

I hate hot muggy days like today because it means that the high humidity will make my hair go all limp and sticky, no matter what I do. By the time I get to school, it's all wet and hanging in my face even though everyone else's hair still looks perfect and great.

Next thing I know, those two boys in my home room start giving me the WHAT THE HELL HAPPENED TO YOU? routine. I don't know what to do. Hairspray just makes my hair stickier.

This led to endless hours staring into those horror chambers of nightmarish lighting and harsh reflective surfaces: department-store dressing rooms.

Eighth grade was life under a microscope. The tiniest social miscalculation could cause a tumble through a trap door into a terrifying landscape of wrong. It wasn't my imagination. We were all being judged and the judges were us. Secret forbidden "slam books" were being passed around that year. When you wrote in them, you kept them hidden. They could be brutal PR for anyone too irregular.

Having exactly the right clothes had become
so critical that allowing my mother to have a say in it,
as she had been accustomed to doing, was
now out of the question.

JUNE 12, 1962

We went to the 163rd Street shopping center and I got a pair of adorable white patent leather flats.

And UGG. Mom made me also get a pair of saddle shoes. I HATE SADDLE SHOES. I DESPISE SADDLE SHOES. I CAN NOT STAND SADDLE SHOES.

This in turn formed a direct link to a serious escalation in a growing war with my mother.

NO ONE looked good in a gym suit. **NOT POSSIBLE.**
That might have been the whole idea. But the cooler girls
with the best bodies learned how to **WORK** them.

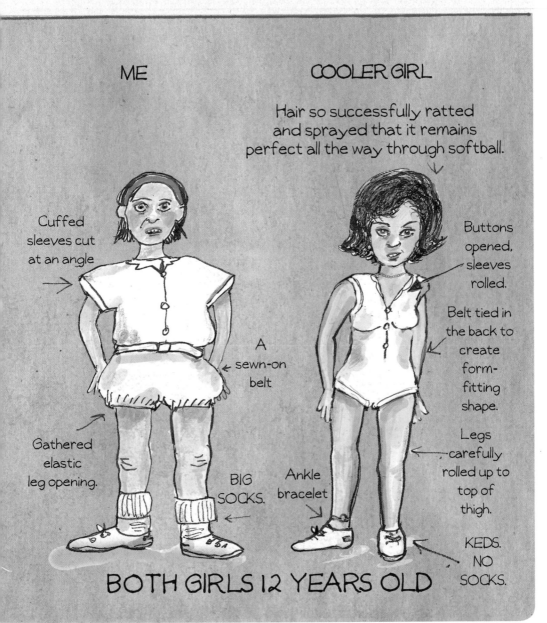

ME

COOLER GIRL

Hair so successfully ratted
and sprayed that it remains
perfect all the way through softball.

Cuffed
sleeves cut
at an angle

Buttons
opened,
sleeves
rolled.

Belt tied in
the back to
create
form-
fitting
shape.

A
← sewn-on
belt

Gathered
elastic
leg opening.

Legs
carefully
rolled up to
top of
thigh.

BIG
SOCKS.

Ankle
bracelet

KEDS.
NO
SOCKS.

BOTH GIRLS 12 YEARS OLD

It seemed like no matter where a conversation with mother started, it ended up with a fight.

JANUARY 10, 1962

Mom practically said bolt out right that she thought I was A TRAMP and a GOOD FOR NOTHING. Why? Because anyone with a different opinion than her own is AUTOMATICALLY WRONG.

If I hadn't reread those diaries, I would have totally forgotten that my mother was a nuanced woman who had more sides to her than simply anger.

FEBRUARY 8, 1962

After dinner Kaye showed up at the front door with Frankie ... sobbing. Mrs. Seagar got drunk again and started beating Kaye. Kaye got her friend to drive her to Freddy Arthur's house. But she forgot her purse. So Mom went

next door and asked for Kaye's purse, but Mrs. Seager slammed the door in her face.

Then Mr. Seager came over, looking mean as can be, and took Frankie home. Now I feel so ashamed of myself for carrying on because I couldn't wash my hair. I HAVE A WONDERFUL FAMILY.

For some reason, only her continuous anger made it into the hippocampus.

Where did you store all the POSITIVE memories of my mother?

Like I found this in November 1962

UPDATE: Please excuse earlier statements, Mom IS A DOLL.

Glenn is still a brat.

Not my department. YOU majored in unresolved anger.

This was the year the ground beneath me grew increasingly unsteady. At any moment, someone who was not even on my radar might open their big mouth and completely ruin my life.

MARCH 2, 1962

Today was a terrible day. In 5th period this girl I have always secretly despised told Mike I wanted to go steady with him. I exploded and told her how much I hate her.

There were hundreds of specifics to monitor. And you ignored them at your own peril. I had forgotten how quickly everything could turn on you.

MAY 12, 1962

Linda's party was horrible. First, I borrowed a muumuu from Kathy because I thought everyone would wear one. BUT ONLY THREE GIRLS WORE ONE!!!!!!!!

To make matters worse, my imaginary social life completely imploded when Bobby had the temerity to hook up with an actual 3D living girlfriend.

JANUARY 5, 1962

It's worth mentioning that Bobby doesn't really mean much to me now. In fact, I think he's A SHALLOW, ANTISOCIAL, PIGGISH HOOD.

I probably would still be nuts about him if he was in my class. But I never even see him anymore, so to hell with that.

More astonishing still was this entry, where Bobby seems to have known about "our relationship," despite having never spent time alone with me, ever.

MARCH 21, 1962

Robert told Andrea I was JEALOUS OF HIM because he is going steady with Marie. AND THAT I'M TRYING TO GET HIM BACK. HE MAKES MY BLOOD BOIL. Plus he's a hood. He gave Marie two passion marks.

Hickeys always confused me. Nevertheless, I wanted one.
You obviously WERE jealous but COME ON! Who wants a guy SUCKING ON THEIR NECK?
It's a sign of love and passion!
ONLY in junior high. I haven't run into it since!
YOU DON'T KNOW EVERYTHING!

I tried to compensate by introducing a new imaginary boyfriend into the cast, but it wasn't the same.

MAY 1, 1962

I have a crush on Skippy but the aggravating part is that I barely know him, which gives me no chance with him. So I'm not telling anyone.

1. Meet Skippy
2. Convince him to love me
3. PROBLEM SOLVED

If anyone happens to see this, like Sheryl, that will be okay because I probably won't even like him by then.

Neither of my parents were too enthusiastic about this new TV-and-boy-obsessed version of their daughter . . . despite the fact that the boys were living in another dimension.

As time went on, everything in, around, or near North Miami Junior High began to seem increasingly ridiculous. The sanest option was to become a smart-ass. So I did.

FEBRUARY 14, 1962

About 2 weeks ago on *The Naked City*, they had an episode about a gangster-type teacher and Mr. Bosco was so insulted that he told us not to buy any of the sponsors' products. He mentioned 5th Avenue candy bars and Luden's Cough Drops. So that's what I gave him for his VALENTINE'S DAY PRESENTS. It didn't make him the HAPPIEST man IN THE WORLD.

How was I to know that the skeptical attitude I was cultivating, for which I was generally punished, would one day be an important tool in how I earned a living.

Went to Lincoln Road like I do every Saturday. We decided to go to a movie. The choices were abominable, so we picked a little gem called *Follow the Boys* because the ads for the movie said it was one of the most HILARIOUS movies of the year. But once it started . . . we were all immediately bored. So I started saying:

4 new HIT SONGS
Connie Sings and the whole fleet SWINGS!

FOLLOW THE BOYS

HILARIOUS story of the GALS who follow their GOBS!

It's going to become HILARIOUS very soon! HANG ON!

Here it comes! Here comes the hilarious part!!!

Damn! I was all ready to laugh!

OOPS. False alarm. Wait. Here it comes . . .

Okay everybody! Get ready to laugh!

We were thinking of leaving early when an usher made the decision for us. These guys have it in for everyone between the ages of 13-18. He walks over to me and stands in front of me because I was on the aisle. "GET UP," he says. I just looked at him.

Get your butt up out of that seat and get out before I throw you out of here!

This is ridiculous.

Ask him what we even did.

Really? Seriously? You're making us leave before THE HILARITY even STARTS?

9: THE CLUB

My prayers for improved social status were answered in eighth grade when I was voted into a secret sorority not sanctioned by the school.

DECEMBER 15, 1961

GUESS WHAT? Last night Andi called and made me promise NOT TO TELL A SOUL but that I was finally IN THE CLUB. Then this morning Kathy had some mysterious secret she couldn't tell me. And later Lynnie burst and told me the news but made me promise not to tell anyone. So I didn't. But when I got home, the letter INVITING ME TO JOIN FINALLY CAME!!

YIPPEEE, I'm POPULAR!

My new sorority sisters were more accomplished than I was. Many had actual boyfriends. I could learn a lot by hanging out with them.

DECEMBER 16, 1961

I went ice skating at the Fountainebleau Hotel for the first time with my friends from the club! We had a great time falling all over the place. Afterwards, while we were waiting for the parents to come pick us up, we were all hiding behind a screen so we could see the nightclub twisters. They kept shooing us away. BUT WE DIDN'T SHOO!!

If there was a greater purpose to the club besides getting in, it was not clear what it was. At first it seemed to be about grooming tips to help us with an upcoming fashion show that never materialized.

WEDNESDAY, FEBRUARY 21, 1962

Today I went to my first meeting. They had this model, Margo, there to talk to us. I didn't like her even though a lot of the girls did. First she starts in going around the room saying, "You're too fat. You're too skinny. You're too fat," etc. Then she says we should go out and buy a lipstick brush and all kinds of other rot.

Then she says she's going to pluck our eyebrows for us. NOT MINE!!

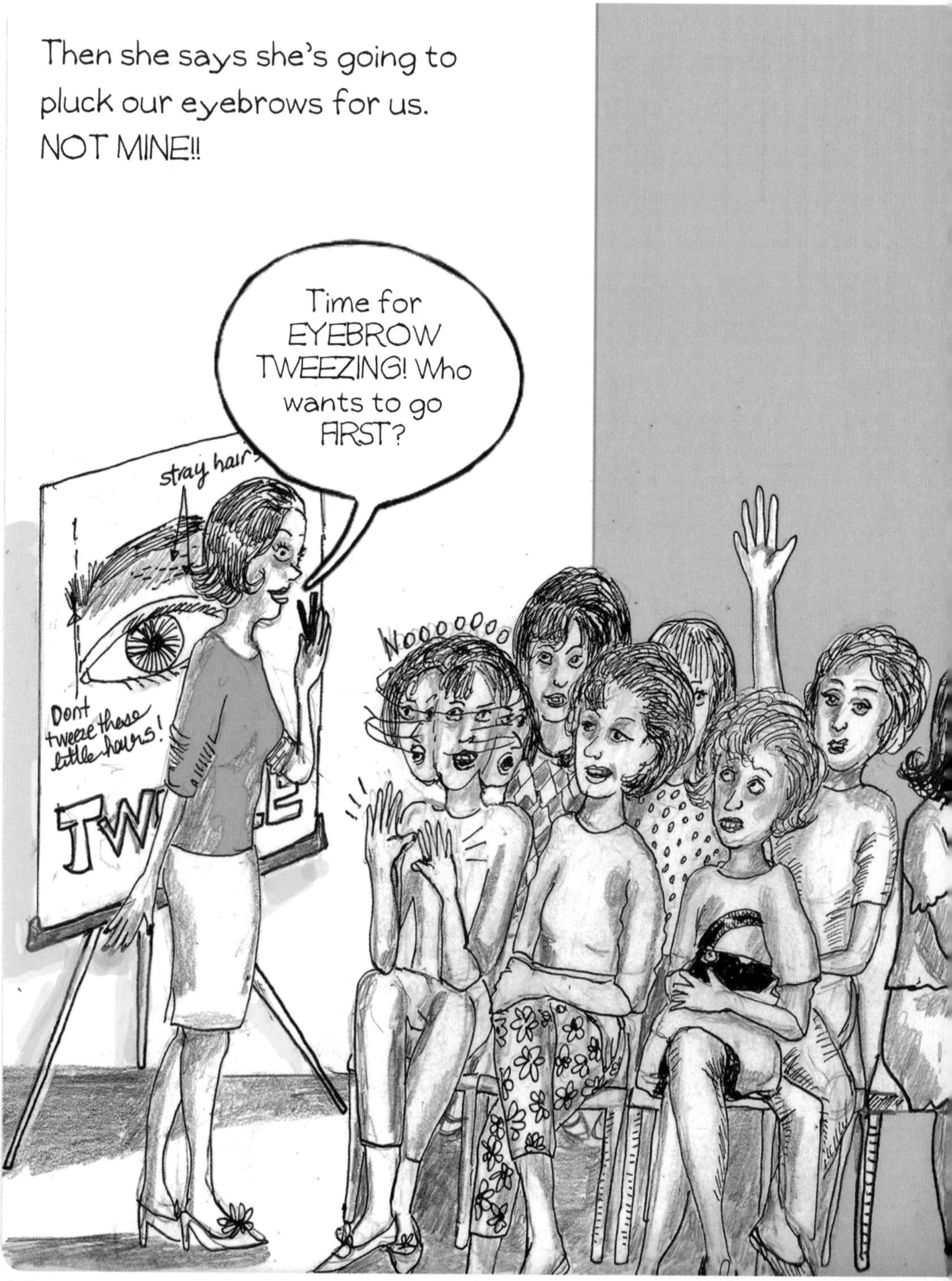
Time for EYEBROW TWEEZING! Who wants to go FIRST?
stray hairs
Dont tweeze these little hairs!
Noooooooo

At the very next meeting there was an attempt to impeach the president. The fashion show was never mentioned again.

MARCH 14, 1962

At night we had a meeting of the club.
We tried to impeach the president.

MARCH 23, 1962

At 1:00 I met with the other girls in the club and we went to the Hope School for Troubled Children to do our talent show. It was all boys. It was terrible. One older boy started grabbing at us. Most of the kids there were so pitiful that a bunch of us started crying. I WAS SCARED. But I think our show made them happy.

One kid made a wailing noise during the songs.

Was he trying to sing along?

Of course we had more on our
minds than politics and civic duties.

MARCH 29, 1962
Our club went to the recreation center next to the school
last night. Most of the time I was on the swings. We put
the seat on our stomachs and took a running start. It was
halfway between flying and swimming in the sand below.

By May, we apparently realized that our important work was nearing an end.

<u>MAY 9, 1962</u>

At night, I went to the club meeting and it was SOO lousy that we disbanded the club early.

In the end, we donated the dues we'd been collecting to our favorite cause.

MAY 26, 1962

Our club had our beach party, paid for by dues. We swam and rested and swam and I got dunked two or three hundred times. At one point I had to go get 6 large Cokes for different kids. When I tried to carry them back, I nearly died because they were spilling all over the place. Finally Howie and Skippy came to get their Cokes and I was saved. Unfortunately I couldn't go to the party at night because I was vomiting from sunburn.

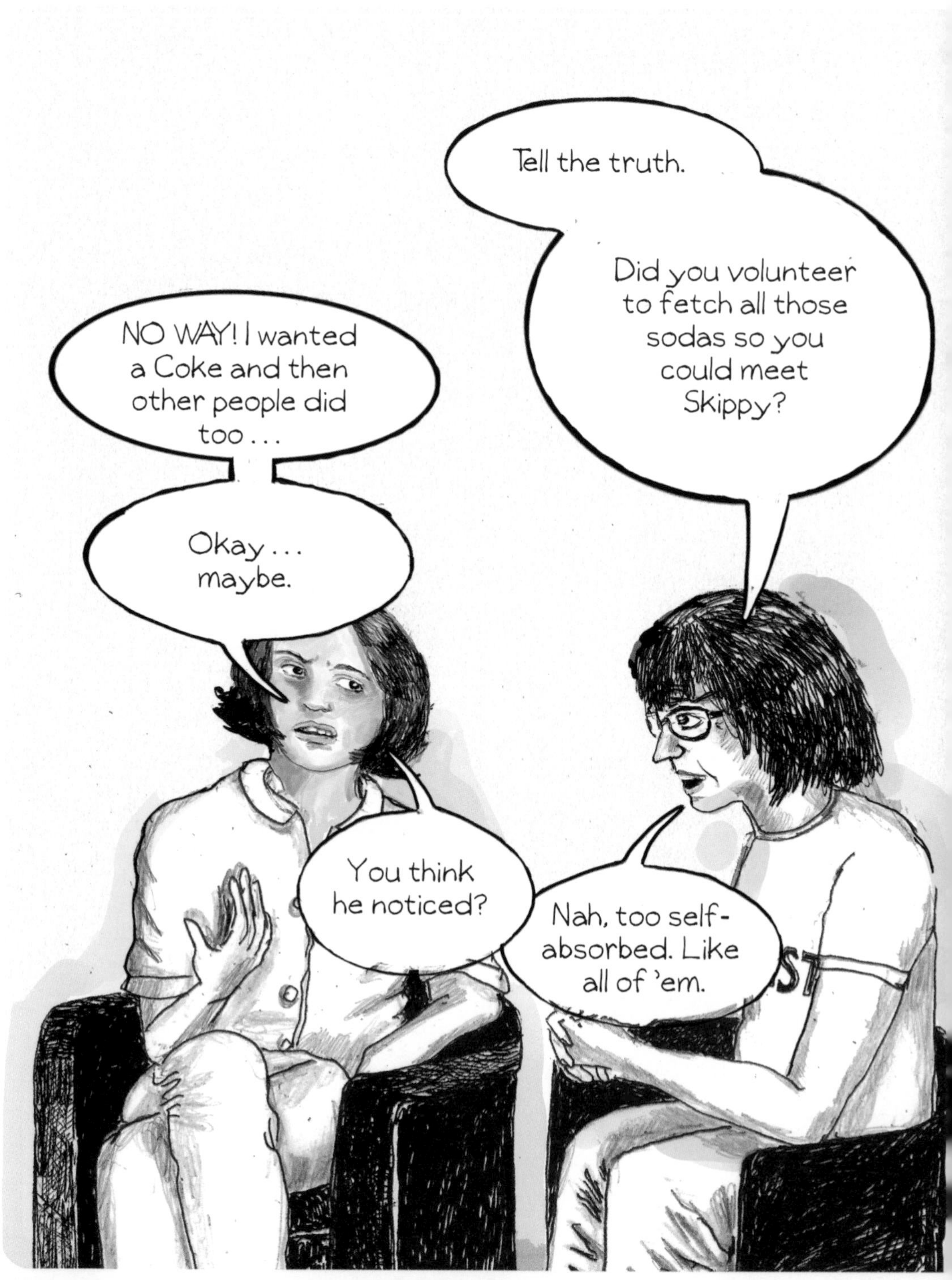
Tell the truth.
Did you volunteer to fetch all those sodas so you could meet Skippy?
NO WAY! I wanted a Coke and then other people did too . . .
Okay . . . maybe.
You think he noticed?
Nah, too self-absorbed. Like all of 'em.

10: MORE WAYS TO BE POPULAR

After the club tanked, my social safety net eroded.

My solution to meeting more boys was to borrow an idea from Lucy in *Peanuts* and open a roadside psychiatric stand. After all, what more tantalizing way to attract reluctant members of the opposite sex than by presenting them with proof that they were mentally ill?

SATURDAY, MAY 12, 1962

Andi and I set up our psychiatric clinic and sat there for a long time without any customers. Finally, we analyzed her sister's boyfriend's friends by giving them ink blot tests, and then announcing that they were crazy. It was sooo funny.

**When insulting boys failed to win any hearts,
I developed a modest backup plan.**

I went to Andi's house and we saw this TV show called
Tell It to Groucho where they fly people to Hollywood from
all over the U.S. to tell him the unusual things about them.
So we wrote a letter to tell him about Perkoe
Psychiatric Clinic. I hope
we can go on.

When that wasn't successful, my next angle of approach involved items I purchased from a joke and magic store. I was very fond of joy buzzers. But my go-to favorite was pepper chewing gum.

JANUARY 2, 1962

I almost had to stay after school in English because I gave Mike Goldstein a piece of my ever-popular hot pepper gum and he couldn't spit it out

because dumb old Mrs. Reid was looking. It was so funny I started to laugh and got sent to the back of the room.

In the story arc of every important historical saga, eventually an even more powerful adversary appears. This year, it was my sixth-period English teacher Mrs. Reid. Many memories have faded, but the smell of her body odor is not among them.

I hate Mrs. Reid. I feel like puking at the sight of her. I got out of sixth period to go to the honor roll party and when I got back, they were reading a story out loud and I missed 2/3rds of it.

So I took out a piece of paper and started doodling. And when the period ended, Mrs. Reid announced I had been given a cut for inattendance. She really makes me PUKE UP.

Actual drawing done in class during a test

I knew we were at war, but if I hadn't reread my diaries, I would have insisted that "she just had it in for me."

.MAY 12, 1962

In homeroom, Mrs. Reid yelled at me because I asked if anyone had change for a five. And she said that was a stupid question. So I said it wasn't really because some kids carry change. Then she yelled at me. .

My part in the ongoing hostilities never made it into the hippocampus. However, it does appear that I may not have been entirely innocent.

JANUARY 10, 1962

I came close to getting sent to the principal's office in English because Mike G. and I bet on how many times Mrs. Reid would bounce forward on her toes and back during class. We almost got caught.

JANUARY 18, 1962

That dumb old hag MRS. REID told me she's keeping me off the honor roll by giving me a C in conduct because when I finish my classwork sometimes I WHISPER VERY SOFTLY TO MIKE, when he's through with his work, too. She's a WITCH and she makes me PUKE UP.

142

That brings us to the point in the story where all the adversaries joined forces to create a united front.

**What was there to do but look for a way
to reach a more appreciative audience?**

JANUARY 12, 1962

At night I was listening to WFUN radio and in the news they talked about how a woman was complaining about the Coppertone billboard with a little girl with her butt exposed. They wanted public opinions, so I called in and they taped my comment and played it on the 7:00, 8:00, and 10:00 news. They called it "a comment from a North Miami teenager."

I think this lady should use her voice to criticize more important things instead of picking on what I think is a cute ad. I wonder what she would have done if the little girl was a grown woman??

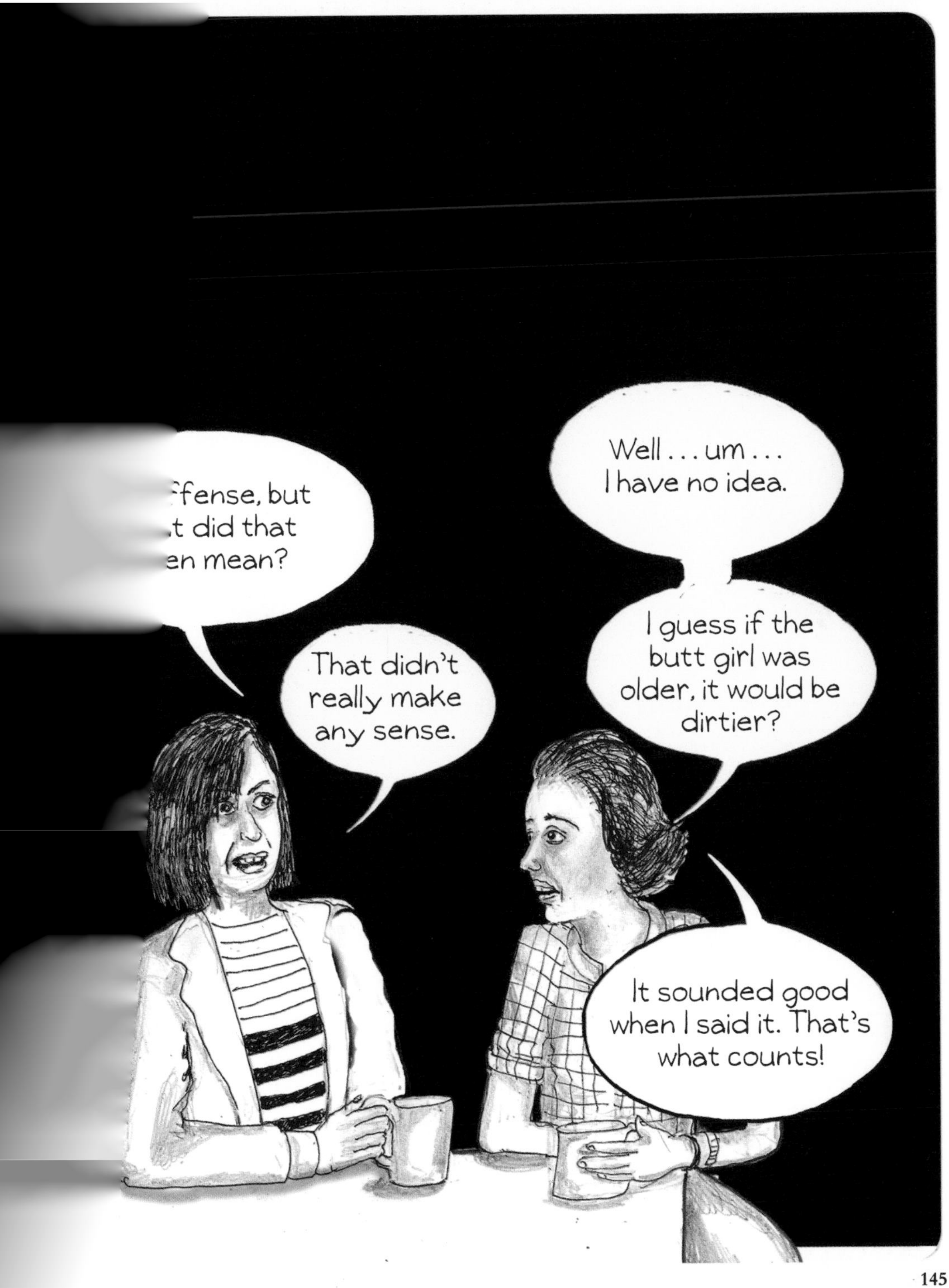
fense, but t did that en mean?
That didn't really make any sense.
Well . . . um . . . I have no idea.
I guess if the butt girl was older, it would be dirtier?
It sounded good when I said it. That's what counts!

11: AND NOW THE NEWS

In January of '62 I began to write my diary like a news report . . . as if to help close gaps in the historical record in the event that my diary was all that was left of civilization.

JANUARY 27, 1962

Today is the day of Col. John Glenn's going into orbit. I turned the TV on at 6:00 but it was delayed so I went back to bed until 7:00 when it was T-minus 45. The DELAY is because of some stratus clouds. I hope they clear up. It's 8:15 and the countdown has resumed. It's a good thing because Colonel Glenn has been sitting in his little capsule for 4 hours. Oh no. Now it's T-minus 40 and holding because of ELECTRICAL DIFFICULTY! TUT TUT.

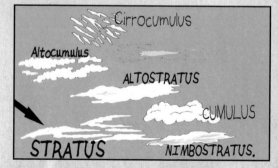

I also began addressing an audience. Sure, it was a nonexistent audience. But all those years of nonexistent boyfriends made the leap easy.

It's about 9:30 now. Or is it? To all my faithful readers, I have some BAD NEWS. The whole thing was postponed! SCROUNGE!

Coincidentally, another Glenn . . . not Colonel but Markoe, is having a birthday today.

As expected, I am not allowed to to attend the party.

In my reporting, I was an omniscient insider.

MARCH 2, 1962

President Kennedy announced
that the U.S. would resume atomic
and nuclear testing in the atmosphere.
I HOPE HE DID THE RIGHT THING!

As general news roundups go, mine got points for an unusual view of the relative importance of the day's events.

SEPTEMBER 30, 1962

Today there was a lot of integration trouble. James Meredith wanted to ENROLL at the University of Mississippi BUT THEY WOULDN'T LET HIM because he was NEGRO so he SUED and won by court order to get to enroll accompanied by the Natl Guard. Governor Barnett of Mississippi got SO UPSET he AIDED the rioting and got taken to court.

In other news, I hate my retainer. WHO KNOWS HOW LONG I WILL HAVE TO WEAR IT?

SUNDAY, SEPTEMBER 30, 1962

I'm glad it's still the weekend because this week was really getting me down and I mean it. I had a fight with Mom because I wanted to pay for an extension phone in my room and she said NOOOO.

Luckily for me, I made this career transition in time to take advantage of the first international crisis I was aware of.

OCTOBER 22, 1962

In the afternoon President Kennedy made a public address. He spoke of the fastly-being-erected USSR missile bases in Cuba and how this could not be tolerated. He said that a quarantine would begin around CUBA and all ships coming in would be checked for offensive weapons. And 4 Russian ships are on their way.

There is a possibility this is the last Monday I will ever see. The next 48 hours will decide if there is peace or war. I feel like crying but I can't.

There's so much in life I've never experienced.
I'll never fall in love or be married.
I'll never have children.
I'LL NEVER OWN A HORSE OR SEE THE REST OF THE WORLD.
I DON'T WANT TO DIE.

Thanks to having developed an attention span that totally matched the news cycle, I was able to conquer my fear of the apocalypse in an impressively short amount of time.

OCTOBER 28, 1962

Andi's party was a scavenger hunt. I got about 3 hours of sleep all night. Everyone was up by 7. We had just started breakfast when Andi's mom began hinting that she would like us to leave. But it was 8 AM on a Sunday morning! No one's parents were even up yet!

NOVEMBER 19, 1962

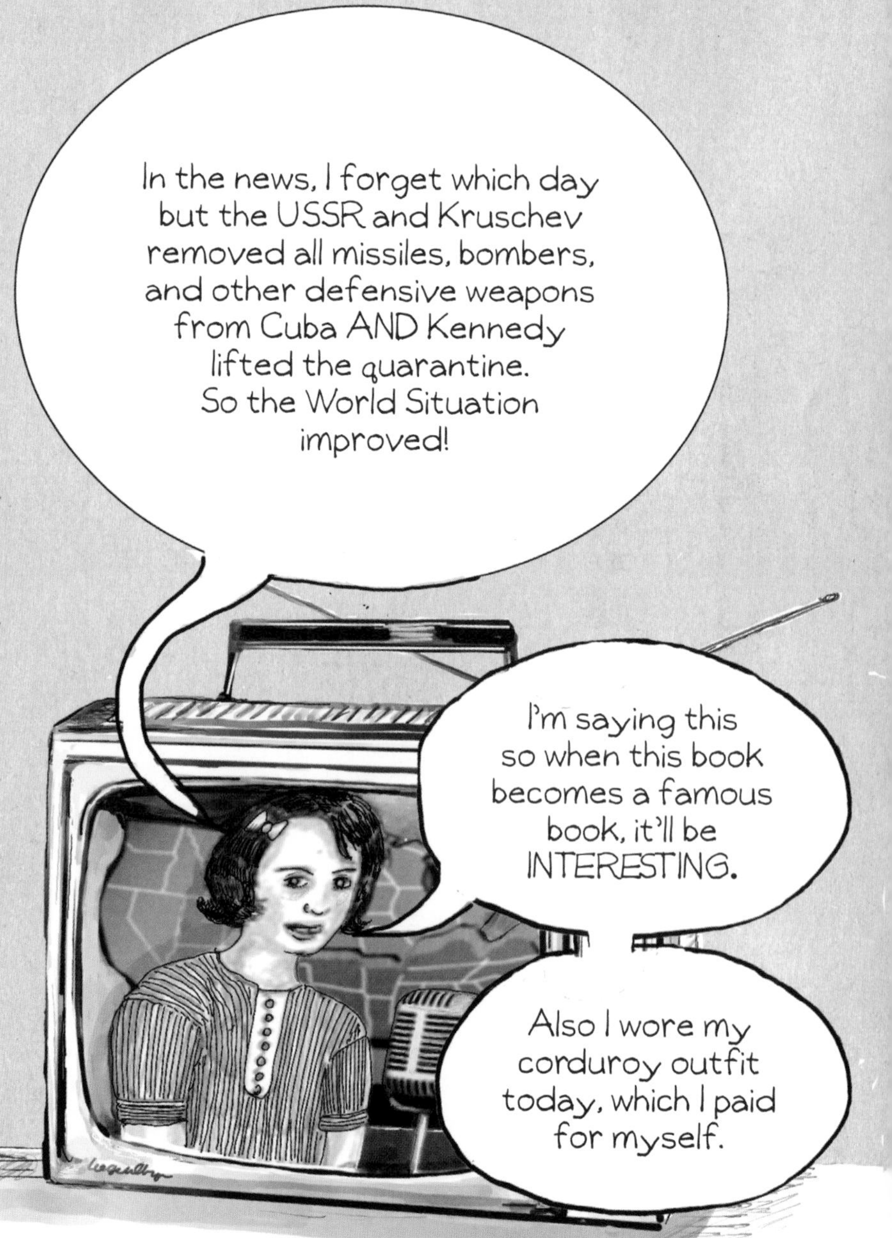
In the news, I forget which day but the USSR and Kruschev removed all missiles, bombers, and other defensive weapons from Cuba AND Kennedy lifted the quarantine. So the World Situation improved!
I'm saying this so when this book becomes a famous book, it'll be INTERESTING.
Also I wore my corduroy outfit today, which I paid for myself.

This broader view of the outside world seems to have started after I went on a class trip to Washington, D.C., despite the fact that I spent much of my time in our nation's capital hiding in a closet to avoid my teachers.

Of course there was more to Washington than closet interiors. There were other dark interiors to conquer . . . like the dank, windowless staircase inside the Washington Monument.

APRIL 20, 1962

At night we saw the Washington Monument, which I climbed 898 stairs worth down the inside of it.

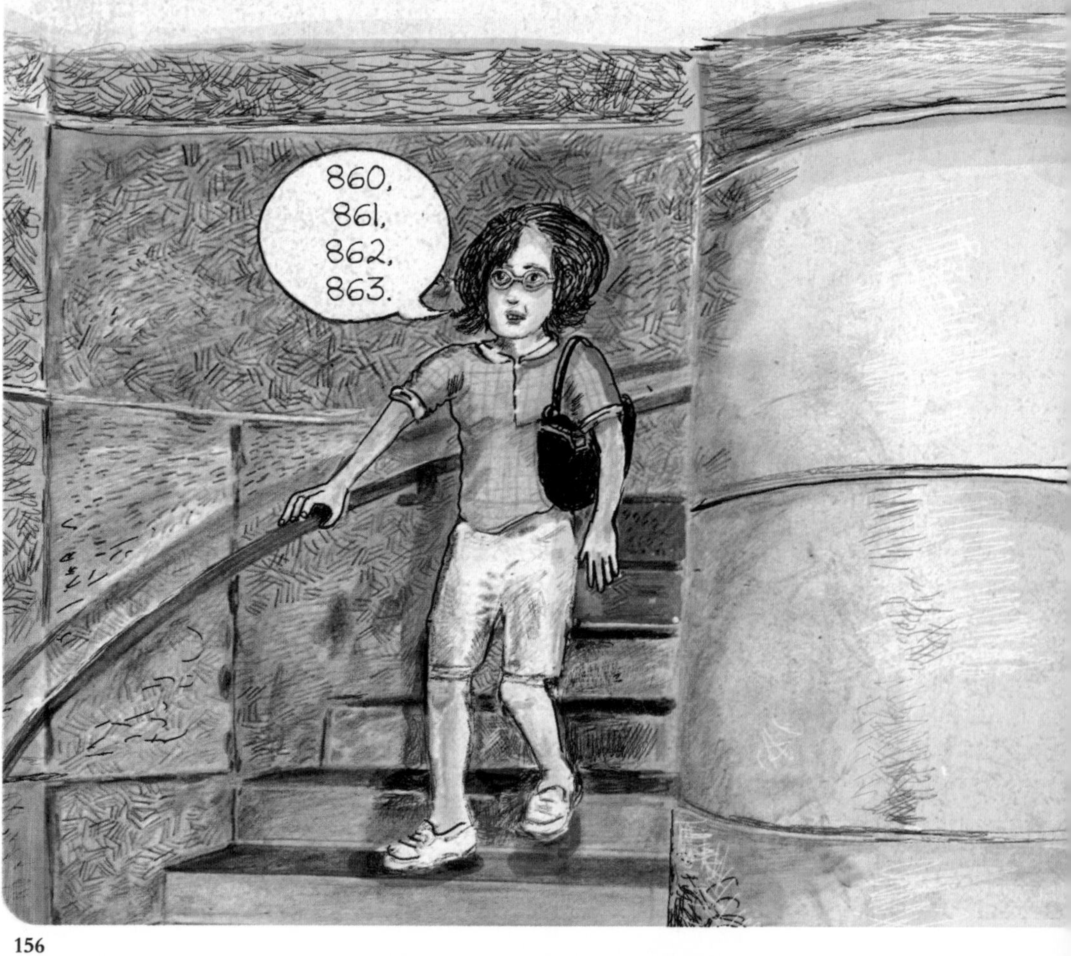
860,
861,
862,
863.

When I came back from Washington, I was so inspired I decided to run for treasurer of the eighth grade student council . . . a position I selected because I didn't think I had a real shot at getting elected president and secretary sounded like a job for someone cuter. My campaign platform, much like my candidacy itself, was pretty straightforward.

APRIL 1, 1963

I knew we had to give our speeches fifth period so fourth period Sheryl R. teased up my hair for me. EVERYONE SAID IT LOOKED CUTE.

I was the third one out to talk. I think it came out all right. On stage I sat next to Carol and Candy. We had a blast talking during the other speeches.

So NOTHING about my campaign resonated as important enough for the hippocampus EXCEPT MY CAMPAIGN BUTTONS? NOTHING????

Well . . . In my defense, everything that was important to you made it in. By which I mean . . .

CUTE!!!

CUTE!

CUTE!

When I lost the election, I was relieved to be provided with proof that it was not my fault. As a bonus, now I didn't have to figure out what a treasurer was supposed to do.

APRIL 17, 1963

Here's the scoop. It's all over school that the election was fixed. Dale heard the principal say that he didn't want too many kids of one religion in office. So when Jewish kids won president, and VP, he decided to have run-offs between the two non-Jewish students for secretary and treasurer.

RIGGED

Now I don't have to do even more math.

Oh well ... Donna Reed is on.

**And then finally, in June, something great happened.
The school year drew to a close.**

JUNE 7, 1962

Tomorrow is the LAST day of school. I just have to say this: Even though Bobby is going steady with Marie, who is very cool, I guess deep down I still like him. I have no idea why . . . but I never talk to him or look at him anymore since that makes him think I'm trying to break him and Marie up.

I'm too busy to notice anything.

I practically don't know he's even here.

The last day of school called for a celebration.

FRIDAY, JUNE 8, 1962: THE LAST DAY OF SCHOOL!
It's the LAST DAY OF SCHOOL. CAN'T BELIEVE IT, I'LL
NEVER GET USED TO THE IDEA! Went to Barbara's party
at 4:30. It wasn't a very good party. But it was an all-girl
party, which eliminated calamities. Except for the fact that
at about 9:00 we heard her dad say, "SO WHEN ARE ALL
THESE GODDAM GIRLS LEAVING?" We felt pretty bad.

Over the summer, I spent a few weeks at another camp . . . collecting more of those special golden-precious memories of summer meant to last a lifetime.

JUNE 30, 1962

At night we set our hair for the big event (?). The first "social" and it was pretty crappy. I didn't get asked to dance once and it still hurts to think of it. I nearly died from homesickness today.

JULY 7, 1962

We had our second "social" tonite and it was as bad as, if not worse than, the first. So Molly and I snuck into the counselor's lounge to watch *The Defenders* on TV.

Frankly, I wish it was Perry Mason.

**There were only a few upbeat memories
that didn't involve horses.**

TV Nite. Our bunk got *Ben Casey*. So Molly and I wrote the play and she was Ben Casey and I was Dr. Zorba. They teased up my hair and powdered it. Everyone said our skit was the best!!

ACTUAL DIALOGUE

12: THE LAST STRAW

Ninth grade was the year my social shortcomings hit critical mass. It was completely obvious that a ninth grade reject was a **REJECT FOR LIFE.**

NOVEMBER 19, 1962

I am 14 and I have never been on a date with a boy or on the phone or gone steady or anything else.

The hostile conditions of this treacherous new terrain seemed to throw everything into question.

First of all, this year the boy situation is terrible. THERE ARE NO BOYS TO BE SEEN. The landscape is barren.

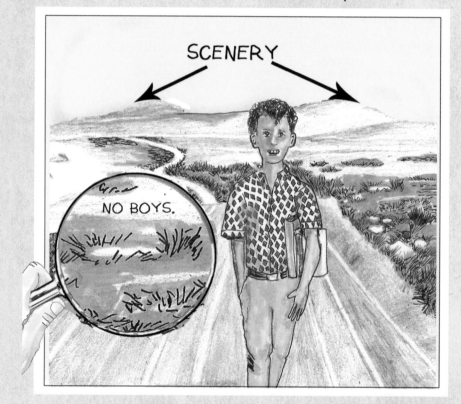

Also, I don't see how I could have liked Bobby in 7th grade. This year it looks like he got a permanent. Ugh.

Things were looking bleak until I saw the movie version of *West Side Story* and inspired me to completely revise my approach to imaginary love. I had seen the film four times. It was a serious commitment.

JUNE 21, 1962

West Side Story was THE MOST FABULOUS MOVIE I'VE EVER SEEN. It's all about 2 gangs, the Sharks and the Jets. There was terrific music, great photography, GREAT acting, and THE CUTEST BOYS! I really liked Eliot Feld, who is Baby John, and Tucker Smith, who is ICE. But I think I like Eliot more because he is younger.

Him!   ME!

I decided that I am going to take modern dancing and become a teenage actress, so I can meet the stars of *West Side Story*. I already know every word to every song.

I tried to identify with Maria, but the idea of singing "I Feel Pretty" and actually believing it felt unimaginable to me.

I knew what I wanted: a sad-eyed, rage-filled thug who could also sing and dance. I wasn't just in love with them, I identified with them.

To show my devotion, I signed up for "modern dance" lessons. That way, when I finally met the boys in the cast, we'd have something to do together on dates.

NOVEMBER 30, 1962

I took my first "modern dance" lesson and I love it. It's so much fun. We're learning a dance to "The Birth of the Blues." I think I'm gonna take it for a pretty long time cause I really like it.

The owner of the studio said Eliot Feld is coming down here this winter and will study here. I found out he is 20. I don't know whether this is good or bad news. More bad than good. Though I guess 20 years isn't so much.

Feels like now is a good time for us to discuss the idea of bending yourself into a pretzel for a guy. Not that you'll ever meet THOSE guys . . . but still . . .
Why are you following me around all the time, trying to kill my dreams?

I was so lost in nutty fantasies about love that when my father's mother moved in for a while, during her divorce, I don't recall asking her a single question about it.

MAY 11, 1962

Mom and Dad went on a vacation so Grandma Annie came over and made us spaghetti and meatballs. Then after, when we watched TV, she kept EXPLAINING the whole show to me like I am 4 years old. She means well but she thinks I don't understand anything. *The Dick Van Dyke Show* is pretty easy to understand.

Then again, the women in my family weren't exactly forthcoming. Both of my grandmothers had poor immigrant parents and ten siblings. Neither spoke about their past. My mother's mother, who lived with us full-time, spoke entirely in clichés. She makes almost no appearances in any of my diaries.

My father's mother, Anne, was an even bigger mystery. She seemed like a woman without a past. Had she intentionally erased herself?
Let's go to Pumpernick's. You can get ANYTHING. Tuna fish. Pancakes.
A dream come true! The full range of human experience.

In fact, she seemed so blank to me that, years later, I tried to get my father (her son) to explain her in more detail.

That was when I discovered that my dad thought having a personality was an optional feature . . . an elective . . . like a stick shift. Or a condiment choice.

No one really understood emotion in my family. If you asked my mother why she was always so angry, she never looked at the bigger picture.

In an unexpected turn of events, October showed real signs of improvement. Things were looking up.

SATURDAY, OCTOBER 13, 1962

The greatest thing happened to me today. I can't believe we finally did it. We finally got a dog! He's a baby beagle and I just LOVE him. We named him Corky and if he ever had to be taken away, I would die. In the evening, I washed my hair.

I didn't suspect that my parents were buttering me up before they lowered the boom.

DECEMBER 1962

Just found out we are moving to San Francisco. My world is shattered. I do not want to move. In fact, I refuse. And I hate my parents for making me leave. Not really. But I am very very mad at them.

At this point both the diary and the hippocampus grow vague. In late spring, when the inevitable cross-country road trip ensued, I was in no mood for scenery.

MAY 1963

By the time we got to Monument Valley and the Grand Canyon, I had seen so much scenery I wasn't that impressed.

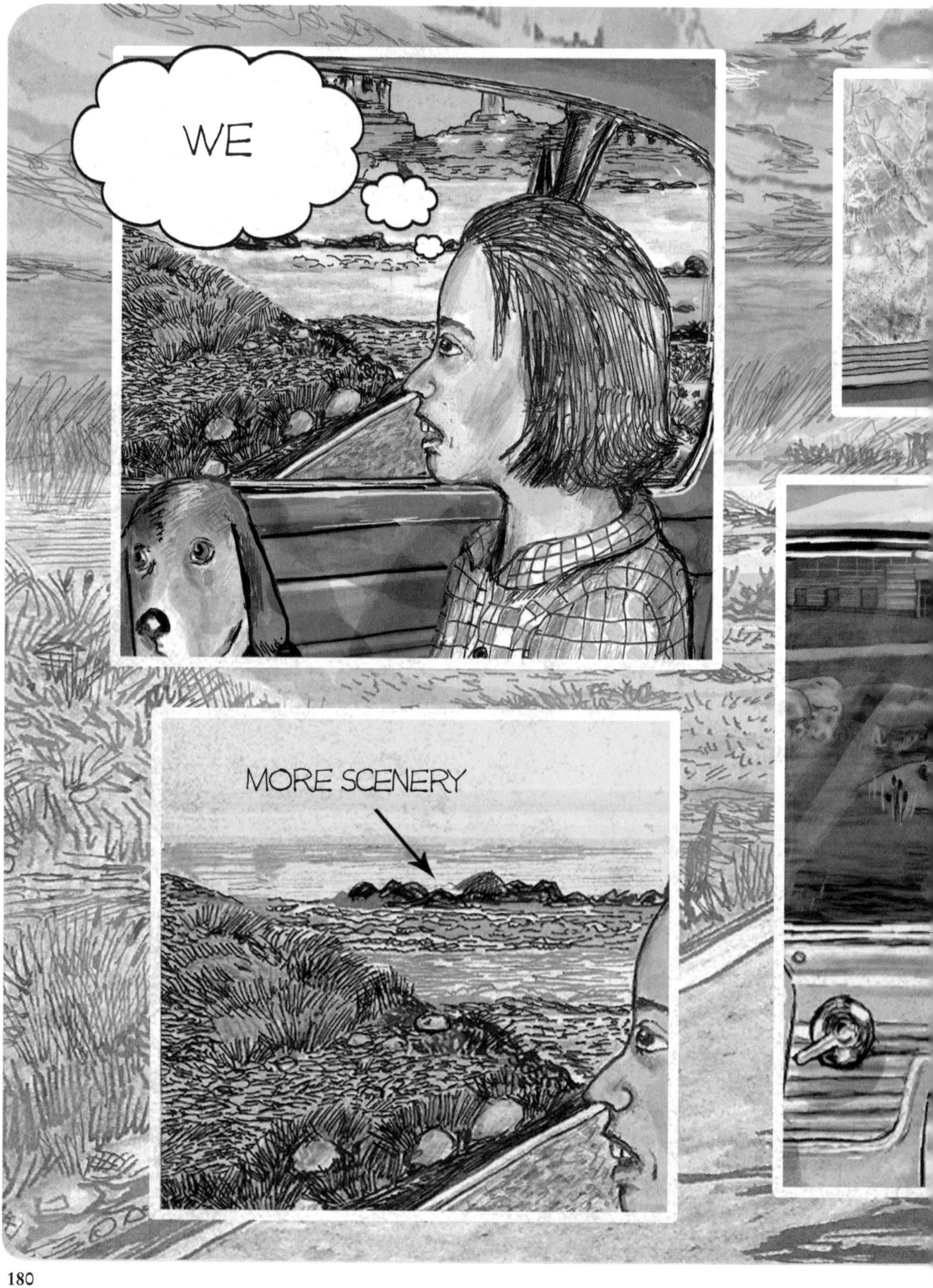
WE
MORE SCENERY

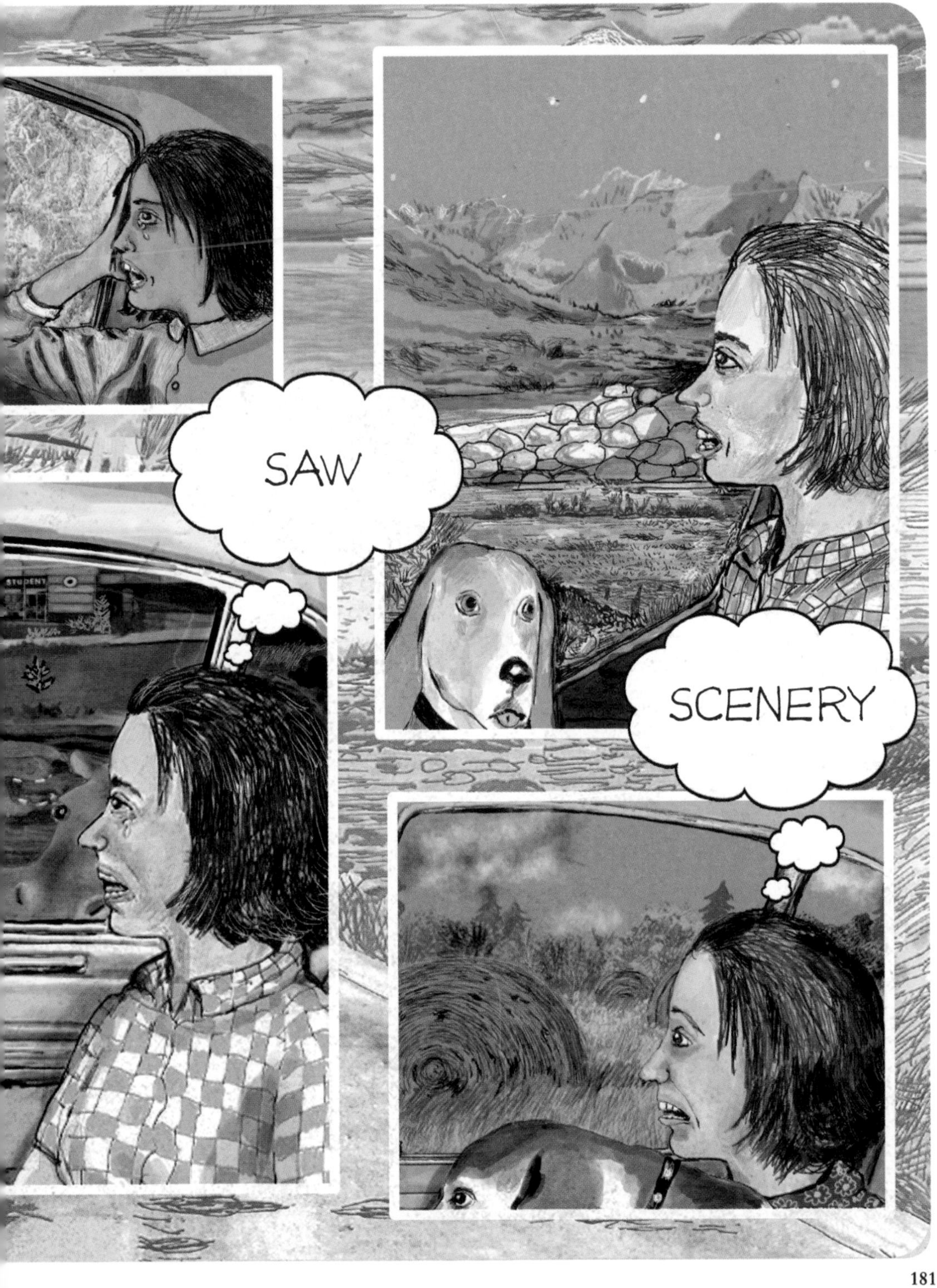
SAW
STUDENT
SCENERY

Of course, once I got to California, my mood brightened considerably.

JUNE 7, 1963

Just came back from walking Corky, depressed as hell. I saw a really sharp sports car come dragging up the road at about 90 with 2 guys and 2 girls all in the front seat, not in that order. Makes me realize how alone I am in this godforsaken place, I HATE IT HERE.

JUNE 8, 1963

I know there must be some people under 70 living around here, but as of right now all I know of is four enormous blocks full of houses where they aren't. Maybe they are hibernating.

In California, it seemed like even the
simplest things had become nerve-racking.

JUNE 20, 1963

We joined a community pool but now I am too embarrassed to be seen in a bathing suit because yesterday my father said "The other girls at the club are certainly very skinny. I see why you want to lose weight."

My dad could be
amazingly clueless.

On the cusp of 15, I knew there was no point in sugarcoating reality any longer. I had become a flinty, hard-nosed realist.

JUNE 23, 1963

As typically teenagery as this as this may sound, my parents actually DON'T understand me. The irony is that they THINK they do because they read some psychology book. But clearly they don't, and all their supposedly "constructive criticism" ... who do they think it is helping? Obviously my tea leaves read "failure" from every angle of the teacup.

Now only one thing was certain: My life was over. Nothing but darkness and staring into the unending void of an eternal horizon lay ahead for me. Nothing left for me but scenery. Forever and ever and ever.

THE END.

PART TWO:
HEADED WEST

13: CALIFORNIA

By the time school started, I was a fount of optimism.

SEPTEMBER 21, 1963
Today was the first day of school. And I realized that to avoid the embarrassment of having to eat lunch alone, I am definitely going to have to skip lunch from now on, because the rest of these kids have known each other since the first grade.

The relaxed, upbeat way my mother dealt with our assimilation into our new environment may have had something to do with it.

Powerless at home and in school, I found strength in issuing national edicts.

Things are happening in the world. Negroes are finally protesting and if they don't get their rights, I will either move out of the U.S. or I will show up at the protests and start cussing at the people who are against them in the worst language. I will show those @#$%%&*!s.

I was FEARLESS. Until an unflattering photo of me and my father attending a big civil rights rally in Palo Alto appeared on the front page of the *Palo Alto Times*.

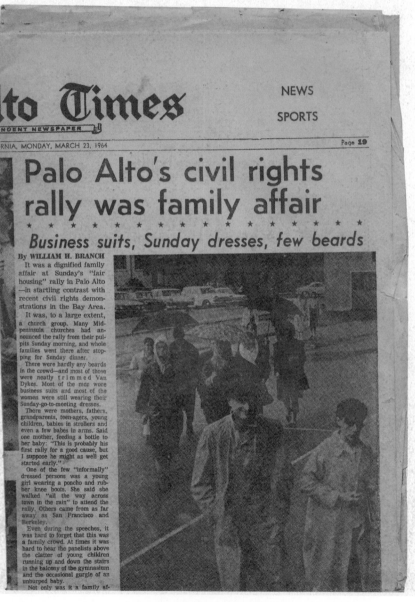

lto Times

ENDENT NEWSPAPER

ORNIA, MONDAY, MARCH 23, 1964   Page **19**

Palo Alto's civil rights rally was family affair

★ ★ ★ ★ ★ ★ ★ ★ ★ ★ ★ ★ ★ ★ ★

Business suits, Sunday dresses, few beards

By **WILLIAM H. BRANCH**

It was a dignified family affair at Sunday's "fair housing" rally in Palo Alto —in startling contrast with recent civil rights demonstrations in the Bay Area.

It was, to a large extent, a church group. Many Mid-peninsula churches had announced the rally from their pulpits Sunday morning, and whole families went there after stopping for Sunday dinner.

There were hardly any beards in the crowd—and most of those were neatly t r i m m e d Van Dykes. Most of the men wore business suits and most of the women were still wearing their Sunday-go-to-meeting dresses.

There were mothers, fathers, grandparents, teen-agers, young children, babies in strollers and even a few babes in arms. Said one mother, feeding a bottle to her baby: "This is probably his first rally for a good cause, but I suppose he might as well get started early."

One of the few "informally" dressed persons was a young girl wearing a poncho and rubber knee boots. She said she walked "all the way across town in the rain" to attend the rally. Others came from as far away as San Francisco and Berkeley.

Even during the speeches, it was hard to forget that this was a family crowd. At times it was hard to hear the panelists above the clatter of young children running up and down the stairs in the balcony of the gymnasium and the occasional gurgle of an unburped baby.

Not only was it a family af-

194

I thought every kid in my class would see the photo and laugh about how hideous I looked. I was horrified.

**Soon the strategies I developed for survival
in this new world put me at war with my parents.**

_____

JANUARY 22, 1963

At dinner tonight my father calmly says he made plans for me for Friday without telling me. They go out Saturday nights so Friday nights are the only night I am allowed out.

Merrill, I want you to leave Friday night open.

Why? That's my night for going out.

I want you to attend the temple youth group.

I'm not even a little bit religious. I don't want to go to religious services.

You're GOING.

NO ONE cares about my OPINIONS.

It was impossible to win one of these fights, since no one ever actually paid attention to anything I said.

I heard what you said, too. You said he doesn't care.

NOT WHAT I SAID. I was talking about being allowed TO HAVE MY OWN OPINIONS!!

You think I DON'T CARE? For the next month I am going to treat you like I don't care and we'll see how much you like it.

That is EXACTLY what you said. I just HEARD you.

My carefully plotted battle plans were routinely tuned out by my father. And after my mother stepped into the ring, all bets were off. A powerful new force field was unleashed.

No. You HAVE NO RIGHTS. This is NOT a DEMOCRACY. We are NOT your FRIENDS. Do NOT treat us as such. Show some RESPECT.

Don't I have the right to stand up for what I believe?

My mother could keep a fight going weeks past its expiration date. What drove me crazy was her lack of consistent logic. Especially since she always had to be right.

JUNE 23, 1964

The next day I was trying my best to forget the whole thing, but Mom kept giving me hell. She is ALWAYS angry. Everything she says to me is delivered in a SCREAM.

WHY are you SO MUCH NICER to your FRIENDS than your family?

BECAUSE my friends seem to like me? Is that anything?

Hey wait a second. You just told me you are NOT my friend.

In retrospect, the move across country was also hard on other members of the family.

JULY 31, 1964

Mom went to the hospital again. Even during our vacation she was sick and in pretty bad pain. What she has is called colitis. I hope it leaves her soon.

From where I sat, nowhere felt comfortable anymore. Especially not in my parents' house.

AUGUST 5, 1964

Sitting here listening to the radio and thinking, "Gee, I sure love rock and roll. There are so many good songs. I wish I had money to buy records but what good would it do? I don't have a record player. My father has a Hi Fi stereo cabinet but doesn't like me to use it. And when I play MY records, the whole family comes in and smirks and rolls their eyes and makes fun of me because all they like is symphonies or Tony Bennett.

Seriously? You mean to tell me you like this?

EW! You like THAT? That SUCKS! How can you like THAT?

AND WHEN I TOUCH YOU I FEEL HAPPY INSIDE
ITS SUCH A FEELING THAT MY LOVE
I CAN'T HIDE
I CAN'T HIDE

My two most reliable new California friends were depression and sarcasm.

AUGUST 11, 1964

Tonight we drove on El Camino and wound up at a place called Chris' SWISS CHALET where we got yodeled at all thru dinner by Swiss cowboys but in those little shorts with suspenders. Every time I picked up my fork, someone yelled YAHOO. Home home in the Alps. Where the beer and the cantaloupe play.

202

As a member in good standing of the prefrontal lobe set, the solution to all my problems was obvious: I needed a cool boyfriend right away.

EPTEMBER 27, 1964

am 15 and I have never had a boyfriend. And if that oesn't seem odd, it should, because I don't know ANY ther girls my age in my predicament and this takes into onsideration ALL of the girls I know of EVERY TYPE. icluding girls with NO PERSONALITIES, STUPID girls, ISGUSTING girls. . . . EVERY girl EVERYWHERE has OMEONE except me.

**Obsessed as I was about being in a couple,
I also had some controversial ideas about sex.**

OCTOBER 7, 1964

Personally I don't get why anyone would WANT to go ALL THE WAY. Maybe I'm ABNORMAL or something. But sexual intercourse . . . the whole idea of it sort of revolts me. It's pretty disgusting if you think about it. The people who do it must be really bored or have nothing else to do.

On the bright side, all my emotional turmoil resulted in a dramatic upgrade in the quality of my imaginary boyfriends.

OCTOBER 1964

f I ever did like a boy, he would have to have A LOT in common with John Lennon. He is the IDEAL member of the opposite sex.

In the seventies Gloria Steinem reportedly said, "Some of us are becoming the men we wanted to marry." Clearly she had been secretly spying on me.

OCTOBER 8, 1964

I am the biggest social failure IN THE WORLD. That's probably why I like the Beatles so much. Because I want to be in love with someone I love John Lennon. He says what he thinks. HE IS THE ULTIMATE ME.

That next summer I somehow came up with the six dollars for a ticket to see my one true love in person. As usual, I was awash in my patented brand of optimism.

AUGUST 19, 1965

When Denni and I arrived at the Cow Palace and were confronted by a group of girls carrying British flags, I knew we were in for trouble. But when the Beatles came out, the SCREAMING was SO BAD it was TORTURE. I had my hands over my ears thru the WHOLE DAMN SHOW! The TRUTH is, we never did get to hear the Beatles. What a VAST DISAPPOINTMENT and WASTE OF MONEY, VERY DEPRESSING. The only thing I actually heard was Paul saying "Thank ya vera mooch."

GOD I hate Beatle fans! Like John would want ANYTHING TO DO WITH THESE IDIOTS. I'M SO SURE!

The place was like
a circus with all the
Beatle junk for sale
and all the sad old
man ushers who were
wearing Beatle wigs.
The emcees were
these cloddy deejays

who kept saying "IS EVERYTHING REALLY GEAR?"
The typical fan was a thirteen-year-old who screamed
right through all 31 minutes of Beatle songs. I was
surrounded by 17,000 of her horrible relatives and
because of them, I never heard one note. Very depressing.

I was so bitter that when a man came up to me, outside,
while we were standing around waiting for our ride home,
and asked me how I enjoyed the show,
I BLEW UP AT HIM!

The next day, as a loving tribute to the outspoken nature of the man of my dreams, I gave his concert a bad review.

AUGUST 20, 1965

Our seats were on the side section but since everyone stood or ran down the aisles towards the stage, Denni and I found some good front row side section seats, which we stood on. At least we could SEE from there.

14: SMOKE

**And then my junior year started. At sixteen,
I remained as happy-go-lucky as ever.**

<u>SEPTEMBER 21, 1965</u>

I hate school. Everything is geared to getting into college, but I have no idea what I want to be when I get out. They say the sensible thing for a woman is to get married and raise a family. But I definitely DO NOT want to do that. I want to be SOMEBODY. And NOT when I'm FORTY and no one gives a shit. NOW.

A bright spot holding the other pieces of my life together in a good way was drama class. I looked forward to it every day until the boy who sat next to me decided to inform me that he could tell I was going nowhere in life.

Last week a boy in my drama class who will probably have a very successful career someday as a nightclub entertainer said to me

Merrill you are great but I get the feeling you're never going to amount to anything. NO OFFENSE.

OF COURSE NOT. I appreciate your honesty. Thank you for sharing.

DOUCHEBAG.

SURE! NO OFFENSE. THANKS A LOT. I HAVE ONLY THOUGHT ABOUT IT EVERY SINGLE DAY FOR THE PAST WEEK. For all I know, he's right. I'm a loser and there's no hope.

Oddly enough, this asshole may have provided the inspiration I needed. Because in the middle of my junior year, I decided to reinvent myself. I made it official by writing a December manifesto.

DECEMBER 5, 1965

I hate people who are prejudiced.
I hate violence.
I hate people who worry
    about what other
      people think of them.
I hate cliches.
I hate people who make
    the same joke over
    and over and over.
I hate people who are
     mean to animals.
I hate MOLDY SUBURBAN
    HOUSING TRACTS
    like THIS ONE.

DEC. 5, CONTINUED

I no longer want to fit in
with everyone. I want
a chance to be
different. In fact, the
weirder the better.
I AM MERRILL MARKOE.
I am my own breed,
my own brand, and my own label!.

JUST DO IT!
OR else DON'T.

...whichever.

Of course some prep was required. I redid my wardrobe and hairstyling choices.

Old simpy plastic me

NEW Nonconformist me

Then I turned my back on my one-time best friend: TV.

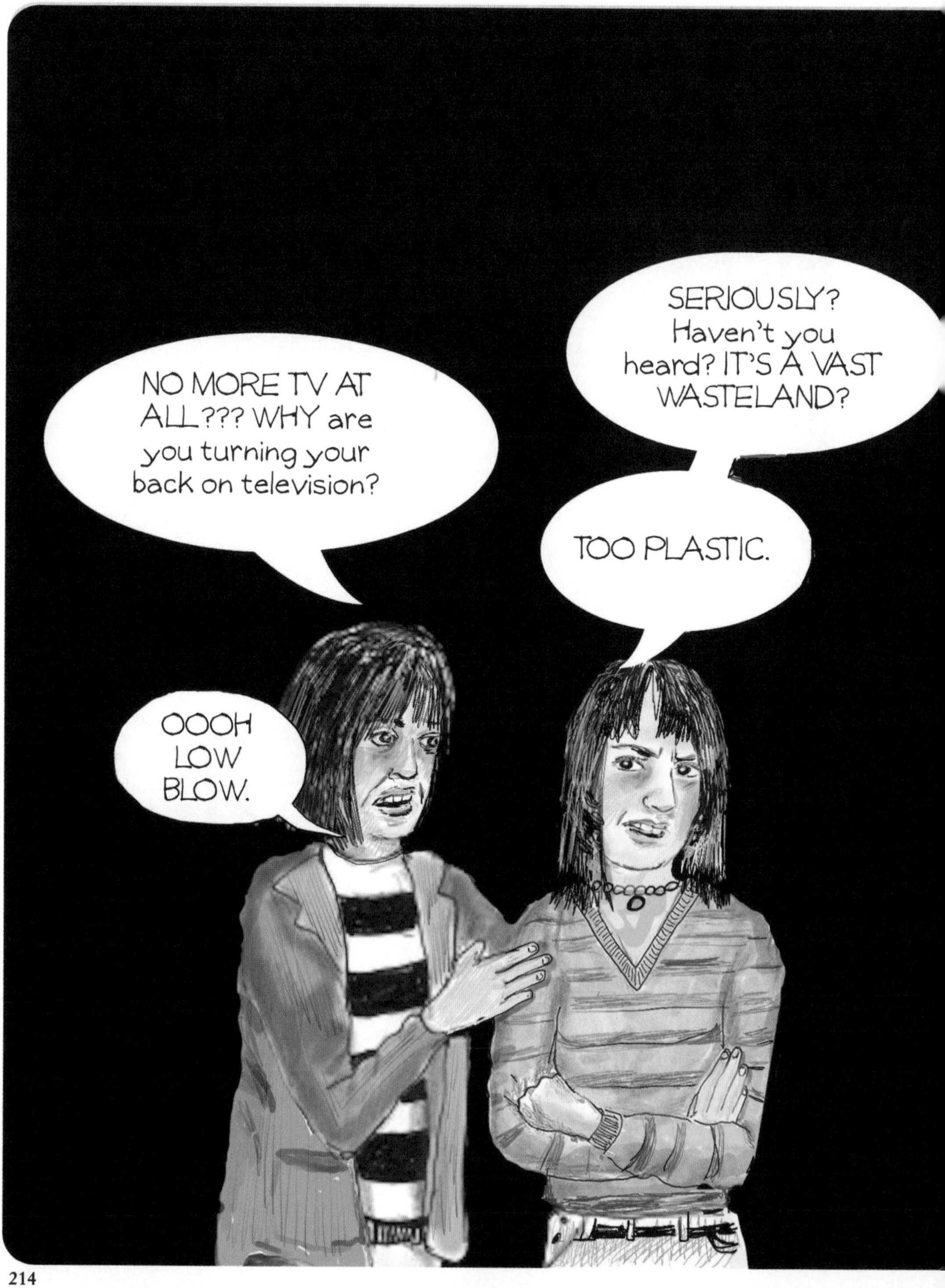
NO MORE TV AT ALL??? WHY are you turning your back on television?
SERIOUSLY? Haven't you heard? IT'S A VAST WASTELAND?
TOO PLASTIC.
OOOH LOW BLOW.

I was trying to become one part Beatle, one part Beat poet, one part smoke . . . a puree of Bob Dylan, Edward Albee, Jack Kerouac, Kurt Vonnegut, and Max Shulman. It didn't occur to me that they were all men. For some XX chromosome ballast, I saw *Juliet of the Spirits* three times.

The new nonconformist version of me was not a hit on the home front. In a related story, I wasn't very good at picking my battles.

JANUARY 10, 1965

I am a very unpopular member of this family again. But living here is the epitome of banal suburbia. The mandatory rituals, like everyone sitting down to dinner at 6:00 whether you're hungry or not, drive me crazy.

Too much effort to sit down with your family? Have it your way. STAND.

ALL I want is salad. So why do I have to sit down at the table to eat it?

You don't get to remake all the rules. You have to sit down.

Don't be RIDICULOUS.

On the bright side, it led me to a new, more creative group of bohemian friends from my drama class. I could not have found them more magical if they'd had wings and left a trail of glitter. Especially after they got busted for pot: a shocking first among kids our age on the San Francisco Peninsula.

I was so thrilled with my new associates that, as an homage to their greatness, I tried to behave as though I, too, had smoked a little pot in my day.

If I smoked pot, I'd probably make faces like this.

My mother found "the new me" annoying at best.

FEBRUARY 5, 1965

A salesman at a store where we went shopping today told my mother that she had "a lovely daughter." My mother replied "WHO? HER?"

Whenever possible, I spent time elsewhere.

<u>APRIL 8, 1965</u>
Last weekend, when Debbi and I went camping, I woke up at sunrise and a raccoon and a deer were about 25 feet away from our sleeping bags. And it seemed so much more realistic than my normal daily life.

15: MORE LOVE

It was a time of great personal revelations for me.
When the new, more subversive me developed a massive
crush on a long-haired artist from another school,
in a shocking turn of events she made actual physical
contact with him a couple of times.

MAY 1, 1965

I have to STOP thinking about him twenty-four hours a day.
It's like I obsess on each incident until it is worn out and
then I think about it all over again. But meanwhile I have
NO IDEA if he feels ANYTHING towards me. I wonder if
I will ever have an actual relationship with ANYONE.
The facts DO NOT look good.

It didn't take me long to realize that he was brilliant. And as a bonus, he had long hair.

SOCIETY IS FUCK.

JUNE 1, 1965

I keep thinking about how this whole stupid society is so focused on trivialities. Just like what Bob said the last time.

He didn't actually say, "Society is fuck" out loud for real, did he?

Yes, he did. And he was right, IT IS.

He had a way with words.

Why don't you shut up?

POINT OF INTEREST:

The rules for a boy's hair length were so strict at this time that any length of hair that was longer than regulation military length was considered rebellious and therefore became an identity definer that bound people to each other.

My long history with imaginary boyfriends did not adequately prepare me for the biological and social challenges I would experience when trying to interact with actual male representatives of my own age group.

JUNE 11, 1965

I have just spent one of the most depressing evenings of my life. Maybe I gained a little insight into things, but I doubt it. Bob and his friend Stanley came over to listen to Dylan tapes. But pretty soon, Bob started lying facedown on the floor, asleep. It's strange, but the more I am around Bob, the less I know about what he expects of me. Or how to act around him.

Zzzzz ZZZZZZ zzzz

Last night at the Pete Seeger concert, when he held my hand really gently, it made me feel like "OH GOD. He is so great. I love him." But then tonight when he was lying facedown on the rug, I just had no idea what he expected from me.
Old Dan Tucker was a fine old man, washed his face in a frying pan . . .

Bob and I did not have what you'd call a "stable relationship." Probably because in the known universe the only things less stable than a relationship with a sixteen-year-old boy are found on the periodic table of elements.

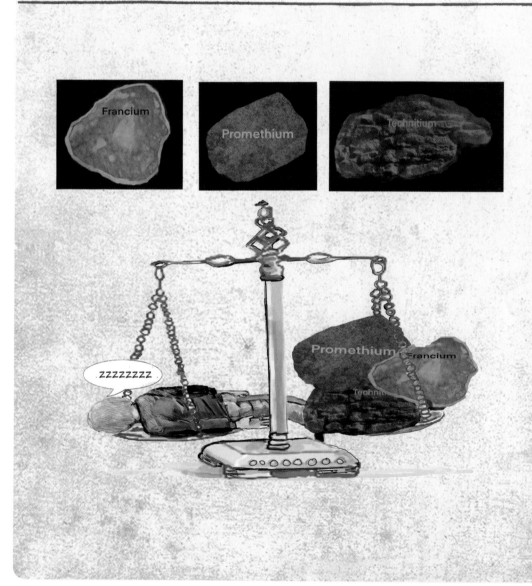

The warm-blooded 3D mammal version of boys was so much more confusing than the 2D imaginary ones I used to conjure.

Then Stanley started trying to put his arm around me. Of course I said NO since Bob was right there. I thought that by ignoring Stanley, Bob would see that I liked him.

I turned the sound up on the Dylan tape, and swear to God this is what was on: "I had a sweetheart and now I have none. She's gone and leave me."

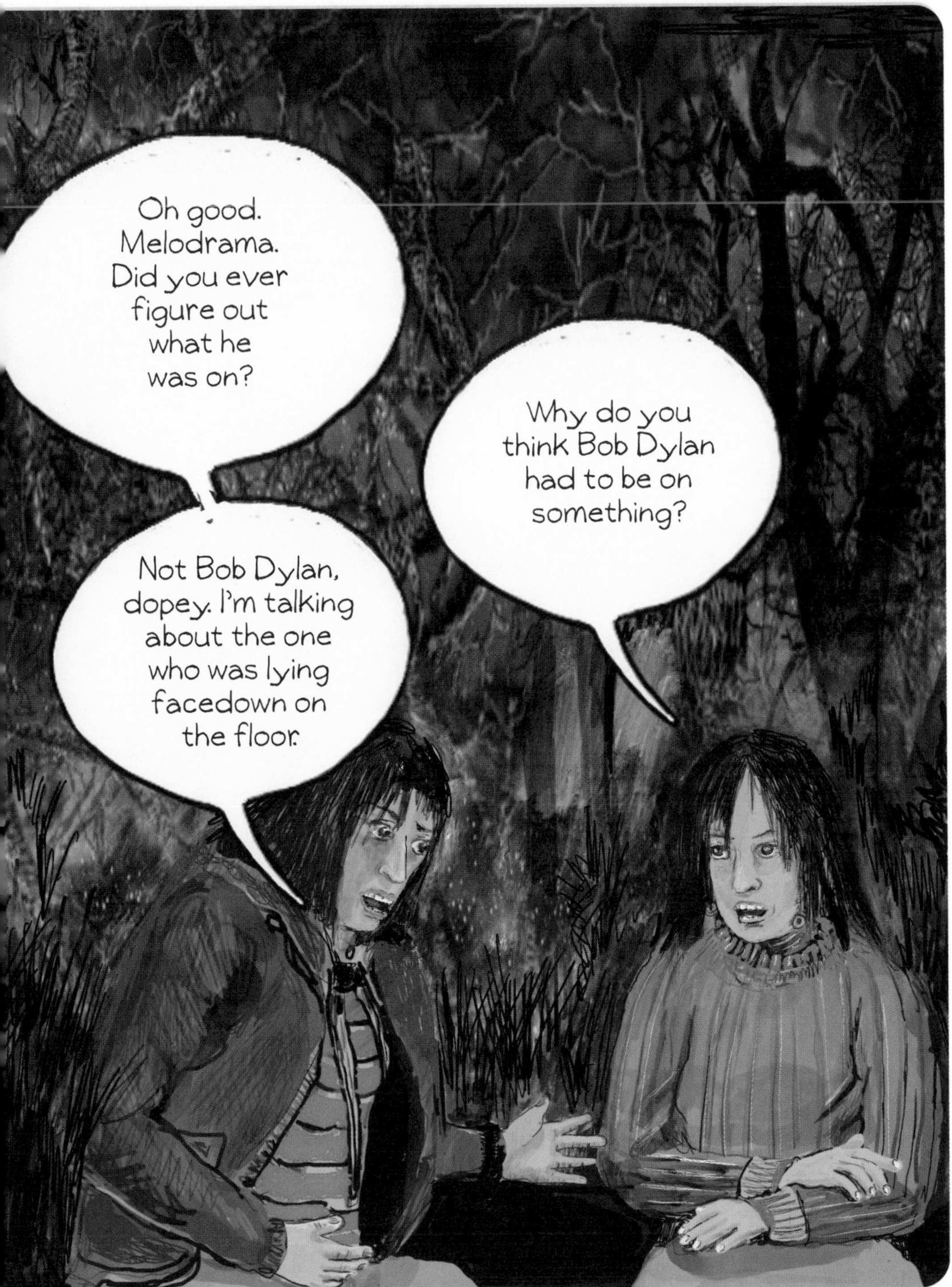
Oh good. Melodrama. Did you ever figure out what he was on?
Why do you think Bob Dylan had to be on something?
Not Bob Dylan, dopey. I'm talking about the one who was lying facedown on the floor.

When Bob woke up, I sat with him for a while but he seemed very far away. I would love to know exactly what he considers our relationship to be. I am constantly wondering what is going on. Am I his girlfriend or just his friend? And if I'm his friend, does he always make out with all his friends in cars?

Uhh. Zzz zzz

So hey! What's up? How ya been? Everything good? Feel like talking about our realtionship?

Sometimes I think (I mean I know) (or I hope I do) that he likes me.

Well, THAT sentence couldn't have been written by you at ANY other age.

Why don't you go back to your own timeline and stay there?

To be fair . . . Bob might have been under an eensy amount of stress.

<u>AUGUST 1, 1965</u>

I just found out that tomorrow Bob goes before the draft board as a Conscientious Objector and I am so scared for him that I couldn't eat dinner. I can't figure out if it's okay to call him. Maybe if I pretend we are just friends it willl be okay.

16: LIGHTS ON

The emotional rollercoaster I was riding traversed more than just my cursed love life. I was also beside myself with worry about the war in Vietnam, "the death of ecology," and "the hole in the ozone layer." The phrase "climate change" hadn't even been coined yet.

AUGUST 30, 1965, MORNING

The more I look at what is going on around me, the more frightened I become. I keep thinking I will wake up one day and it all will have stopped right in its tracks. It seems like things are reaching the point of no return.

It couldn't have been easy for anyone living with me on my crazy seesaw of emotions.
One day I was UP.

SUNDAY, AUGUST 22, 1965

I am happy to announce that I now am finally over Bob and I feel like a NEW PERSON! I have so much energy that I want to run up and down the street. Only 2 days ago I was ready to slit my wrists. But now I want to get in a car and see and do everything. Plus my family seems to like me again. That's good.

WWheeeeeeeeeeeee

AND THEN something would happen that would send me caroming 180 degrees in the other direction. *BOOM*. I'd crash back down.

AUGUST 29, 1965

I can't stand to hear about love now. It all seems like a big fake. Now that I've had ONE boyfriend, I've FINALLY learned something. It's not in my interests to ever love ANYONE EVER AGAIN. Everything is bleak and horrible.

Meanwhile, in a related story: MY RELATIONSHIP WITH MY MOTHER CONTINUED DETERIORATING.

JULY 1965

Tonight before I went to my musical theater workshop, my mother said that she and my father had given up all hope for me because I had become everything they hoped I would not. So now they no longer cared about what happened to me because I had become a Frankenstein monster.

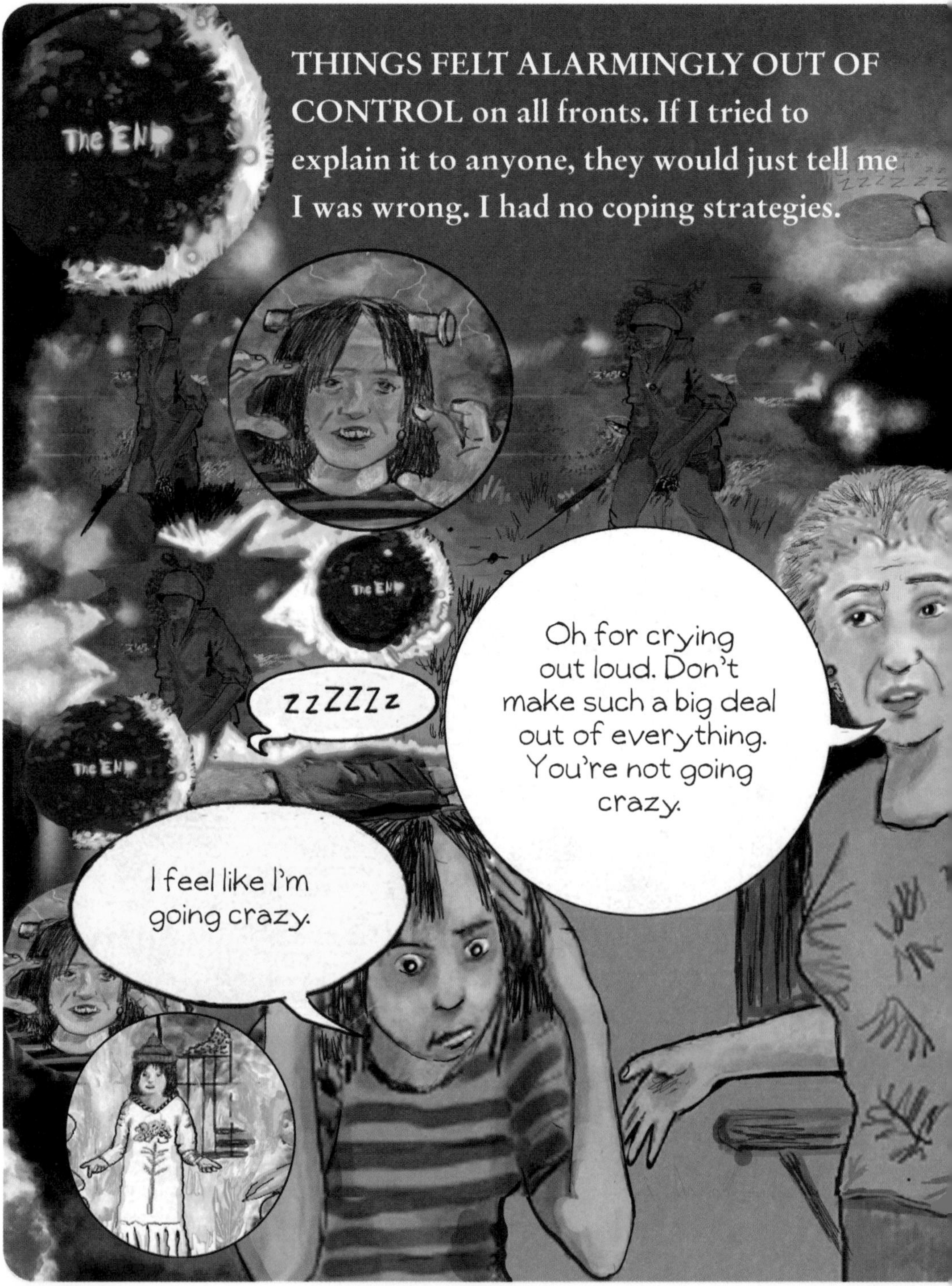
THINGS FELT ALARMINGLY OUT OF CONTROL on all fronts. If I tried to explain it to anyone, they would just tell me I was wrong. I had no coping strategies.
zzZZZz
Oh for crying out loud. Don't make such a big deal out of everything. You're not going crazy.
I feel like I'm going crazy.

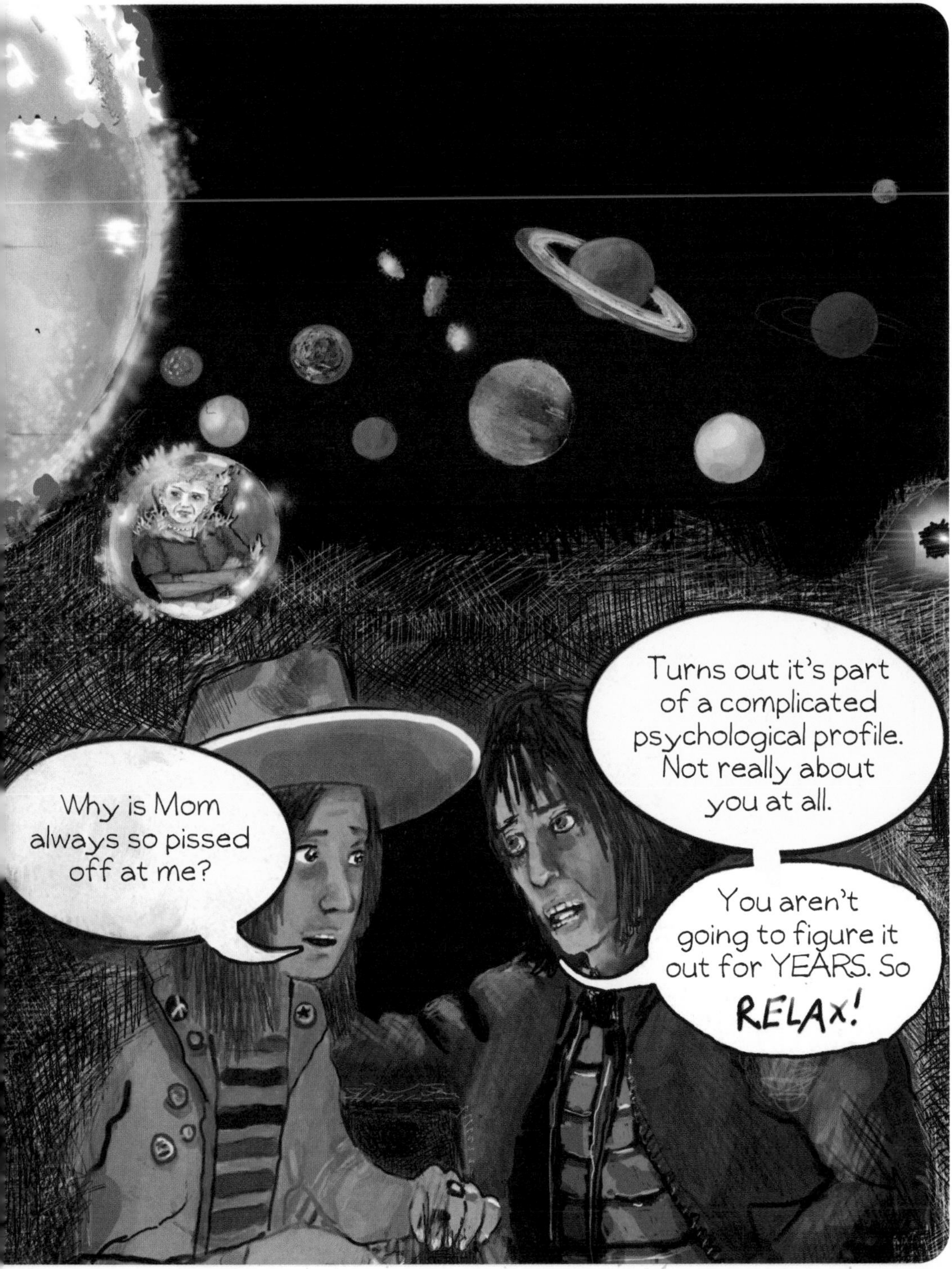
Why is Mom always so pissed off at me?
Turns out it's part of a complicated psychological profile. Not really about you at all.
You aren't going to figure it out for YEARS. So RELAX!

By now, even the universe was fed up with my mood swings, so it decided to give everyone a break and turn the light on.

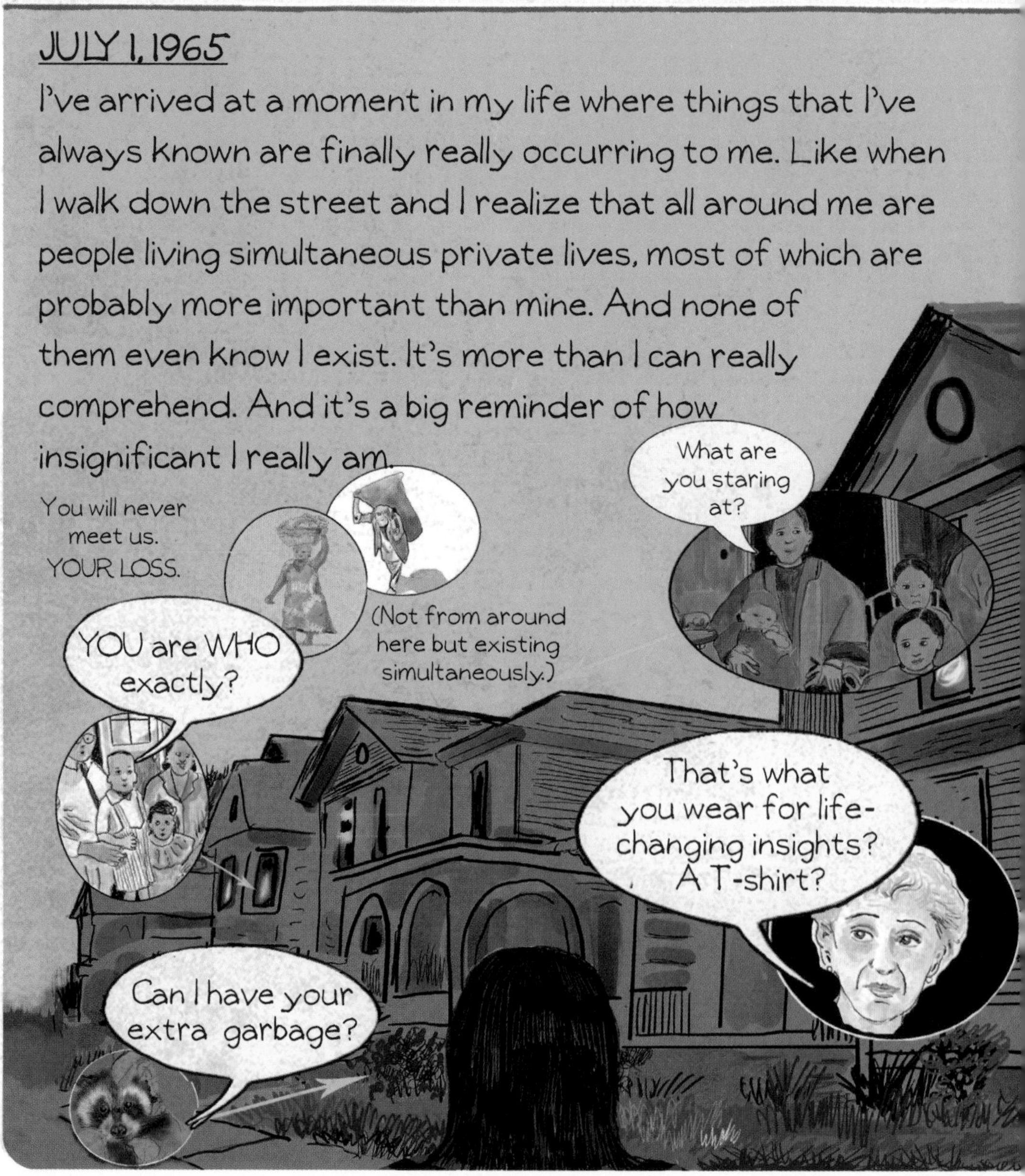
JULY 1, 1965
I've arrived at a moment in my life where things that I've always known are finally really occurring to me. Like when I walk down the street and I realize that all around me are people living simultaneous private lives, most of which are probably more important than mine. And none of them even know I exist. It's more than I can really comprehend. And it's a big reminder of how insignificant I really am.
You will never meet us. YOUR LOSS.
(Not from around here but existing simultaneously.)
What are you staring at?
YOU are WHO exactly?
That's what you wear for life-changing insights? A T-shirt?
Can I have your extra garbage?

17: RESCUED BY ART

It occurred to me that I had two choices: 1. I could sink under the weight of how depressing things were . . . which was happening more and more.

NOVEMBER 30, 1964, RIGHT BEFORE BED

I guess it's a good thing that an extremist like Barry Goldwater was defeated in the last election. That was SCARY. But it's still driving me crazy that Proposition 14, which repealed the Fair Housing Act and legalized hatred and bigotry in California, PASSED. WHY ARE PEOPLE SO STUPID?

Or 2., I could try to handle things like I had seen Wile E. Coyote do on numerous occasions: by painting a tunnel on a solid rock wall, and escaping into it.

Rethinking the world as comedy was like a magic trick where I was in control. I could turn something I didn't like into something I liked a lot. It was like an escape tunnel.

Being creative made me feel like I was in charge of the structure of my world. It was an excellent escape route.

JUNE 10, 1965

I came up with a list of things I had never seen made into stuffed animals. And then Debbi and I made them out of drawings I did on felt: a radish, a plate of fried eggs, a can of V-8, a potato. We stuffed them with foam rubber. And then Debbi dressed them in little leather coats and boots.

Almost by accident I had started a small business trying to make money selling our stuffed animals.

AUGUST 10, 1965
Debbi and I walked all over San Francisco trying to make money selling our stuffed animals. Some old guy yelled "Hey Daniel Boone" at us, but by the end of the day we sold 16 of them to a store in the Haight.

What time does the cattle drive leave?

About the same time the bar where you're headed opens.

The new, more subversive me started submitting anonymous letters to the school paper, which had recently taken a stand against student activism.

Dear Mr. Editor,
I have a remedy to suggest how to help our school deal with the problem of young people who do not agree with U.S. policies. Why not hold a mandatory costume competition, where all the students, grades 10-12, must come dressed as their favorite national monument? Such an activity would help instill patriotism in these young people during these important years when they are molding.

I also began writing a novel where I tried to portray myself as Holden Caulfield. But since I had little in common with him, and also no idea who I was . . . clearly that was not going to work out. I could tell you the name of the novel but . . . too embarrassing.

Okay, okay . . . It was
The Cheese Stands Alone.
You happy now?

Around this time, my reason for keeping a diary changed. Instead of a record of the day's events, it became a hideout where I went to cope with overwhelming things.

JULY 3, 1965

I think the reason I like to write is because I notice that even when I am experiencing bad things, I still like watching all the phases I go through. It's interesting to see where they all lead.

Here's the thing: people are insane!

And then hooray! I finally started having
fantasies about something besides boys!
Although I admit the symbolism was eerily similar.

JULY 6, 1965

If I could decorate my room however I wanted, I would
install stalagmites and stalactites. GOD! That would be
the ultimate room decor.

Absurd.

Don't be ridiculous.
Under no circumstances
would I ever agree to
allow you to fill your
room with stalactites.

That summer I really hit pay dirt when I somehow got accepted into a class for high school students at the San Francisco Art Institute.

JULY 22, 1965
This morning I went to my class at the San Francisco Art Institute. I made the bike ride to the train station in record time.

I took the 7:30 train. On the way, I read a couple of chapters of Kerouac's ON THE ROAD. And here's what I took from it: I REALLY need to get out and absorb a lot more of EVERYTHING. I think I have been vegetating for 16 years.

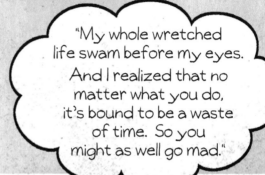

Everything about that experience, including all the different forms of transportation it took to get there, made me feel like a much cooler person.

Unfortunately, I painted badly today. I did a still life and got carried away using browns and blacks until it got all muddy because I was distracted trying not to think about Bob. I've never been jilted before. But then, I've never really liked anyone before. I finally poured turp over the whole thing, smeared it and in bright yellow I drew a perturbed girl and wrote the word HELP.

JULY 4, 1965

More and more I have been feeling obsessed by the need to write about how things are. I have been realizing that I am kind of a funny girl. I don't know if that is a special thing. And if it is I don't know what category it puts me in.

It wasn't clear to me that being funny was a thing of any value. When I said something I thought was funny around my family, it usually felt like I had done something wrong.

**My relationship with my parents
was very tense during this period.**

JULY 10, 1965

My father says he dislikes my appearance, my attitude
about independence, and my taste in almost everything.
He says people see me as a clown. That they laugh at me
and see me as "silly."

This was the summer I learned that when things seemed funny, it was a good idea to immediately write them down in a notebook.

18: LET'S GET OUT OF HERE

My parents watched me warily. I don't know what they were so worried about.

<u>SUNDAY, AUGUST 8, 1965</u>

I just had the most horrible horrifying disgusting experience. I can't live with myself anymore. I want to die. Last night I went to a party at Melvin's and I wanted to get drunk enough to experience it.

AUGUST 8, 1965 CONT.

I guzzled some beer but I couldn't tell if I was drunk or not. So I drank an 8-ounce glass of vodka. I can't remember much else except at one point I was rolling around on the floor with Bob and when Debbie drove me home, the last thing I said when I got out of the car was "The only person who knows what's going on is Jean Paul Sartre."

NICELY DONE! You might be a writer after all.

How'm I doin', Jack?

Oh hi, Mom.

Do you have Sartre's phone number?

By the time I saw my parents, it was 4:30 a.m. And the first thing Mom yells at me is "Whose clothes are you wearing?" That was the first time I realized I had no idea whose clothes I had on. So of course now she thinks I slept with someone. But I know I didn't. I found out that what happened was I was barfing all over everything and Debbi went and found some clean clothes for me.

Now my parents hate me again.

Today I found a quote from Jean-Paul Sartre which I made into a sign to hang in my bedroom. "Man will be nothing unless he has first understood that he must count on no one but himself; that he is alone, abandoned on Earth in the midst of his infinite responsibilities."

Luckily for me, my growing devotion to being creative gave me more of a center than my growing devotion to drinking. It even helped me find a boyfriend who was able to remain fully conscious during our dates.

DECEMBER 1, 1965

Jeff is a wonderful, kind, patient, stable human being who for some reason loves me. So naturally my mother says he's a psychopath. I love my parents but lately they have become unbearable.

What are your plans for after graduation?

Which of the most commonly used blunt instruments do you currently prefer?

> Despite my mother's fear and paranoia, the truth was Jeff and I weren't even sleeping together.

DECEMBER 15, 1965

Jeff's mom was passed out drunk so he came over with the car. I suggested we drive around and check out the Christmas lights. I guess he didn't like that idea because every time we came to a house that had even one light on it, he'd pull into their driveway and start shouting like it was so amazing until I was cringing with embarassment.

Okay, Mom had it wrong. He wasn't a psychopath. But I feel compelled to tell you that you are embracing humiliation as endearing. Which doesn't bode well for you in the future.
Ever hear of living for today? You're as out of it as Mom.
HEY! I'm giving you points for no Nazi salute.

We did go on some entertaining dates. And it's a good thing I had learned to write all the interesting stuff down because this street guy's great line, which made it into my diary, never made it into the hippocampus.

SUNDAY, DECEMBER 19, 1965

Jeff and I walked through an empty section of Market Street where, this being Sunday when God-fearing Christians are in church, a Negro woman asked me if I had been reborn yet and handed me a religious pamphlet. I was reading it out loud to Jeff when I noticed a bunch of guys on the sidewalk were listening to me. "Go on," one of them said to me, "Read if you want to but . . ."

You can't convert me. I ain't one of them convertibles.

STUDENT CENTER
THAT was a GREAT line. WHY didn't we save it?
We needed the space for those gory images from horror movies where you closed your eyes but actually were peeking through your fingers.

Obviously the hippocampus gave the Ken Kesey Acid Test its own special conference room. Yes, I attended this legendary hippie era event full of sixties luminaries, but I only had eyes for the most important person there.

JANUARY 8, 1966

Went to Longshoreman's Hall in SF to see THE KEN KESEY ACID TEST. There were wild people dancing. There were strange, blinking lights, gold balloons, flying saucers, huge bags of popcorn, home movies of Ken Kesey, and "Batman" projected onto a wall. There was phosphorescent paint all over everyone, pot everywhere, and a huge piece of sheet metal with a thousand people banging on it.

There was a band called the Warlocks playing really loud. BUT MOST AMAZING OF ALL: I SAW BOB!! BOB!! BOB! We will get back together again some day. I know it.

Because I had zeitgeist blindness, I proudly embraced my place in history as the only person to leave the acid test early.

It was too late. By now I had turned into a version of the adult that I would become: Someone who buys tickets to hip events and then always wants to leave early.
I know, I should love "Burning Man." But . . . can we get out of here? Like now?

sh I could say I became smarter about handling love
tionships, but a lifetime consumption of books and
ies had taught me some very bad ideas about how it
all supposed to work.

20, 1966

p having dreams about sleeping with someone who
ved such a tough life he is afraid to be vulnerable and
ehow I am the only one who can get through to him. I
ue them and we turn
o be funny and
t together.

267

You're not going to like this but... THAT IS SO FUCKED UP.
So now you're going to try and convince me that there's something wrong with rescuing someone?
Depends. Works great as long as it's an injured baby animal.
Every single thing I do is a problem for you, isn't it.
Uh oh. That means you're not listening.

High school graduation turned out to be more deadly skirmishes in the unending ground war with my family.

<u>JUNE 20, 1966</u>

I was ready to leave for graduation when my father walked in and told me I could not leave the house wearing my regular school clothes. I argued,

They're PAINFUL. You get to wear comfortable shoes. Why can't I?

DON'T BE A SMART-ASS.

"Why does it matter? Everything will be covered up by a long robe." He said, "Just because your friends dress sloppy doesn't mean you have to. We have enough money for you not to." Then he said if I wore regular clothes, he might not attend.

So I went back in and changed into that hideous dressy outfit and those horrible shoes and I felt ludicrous. And then after the ceremony was over, I found out that neither of my parents even attended.

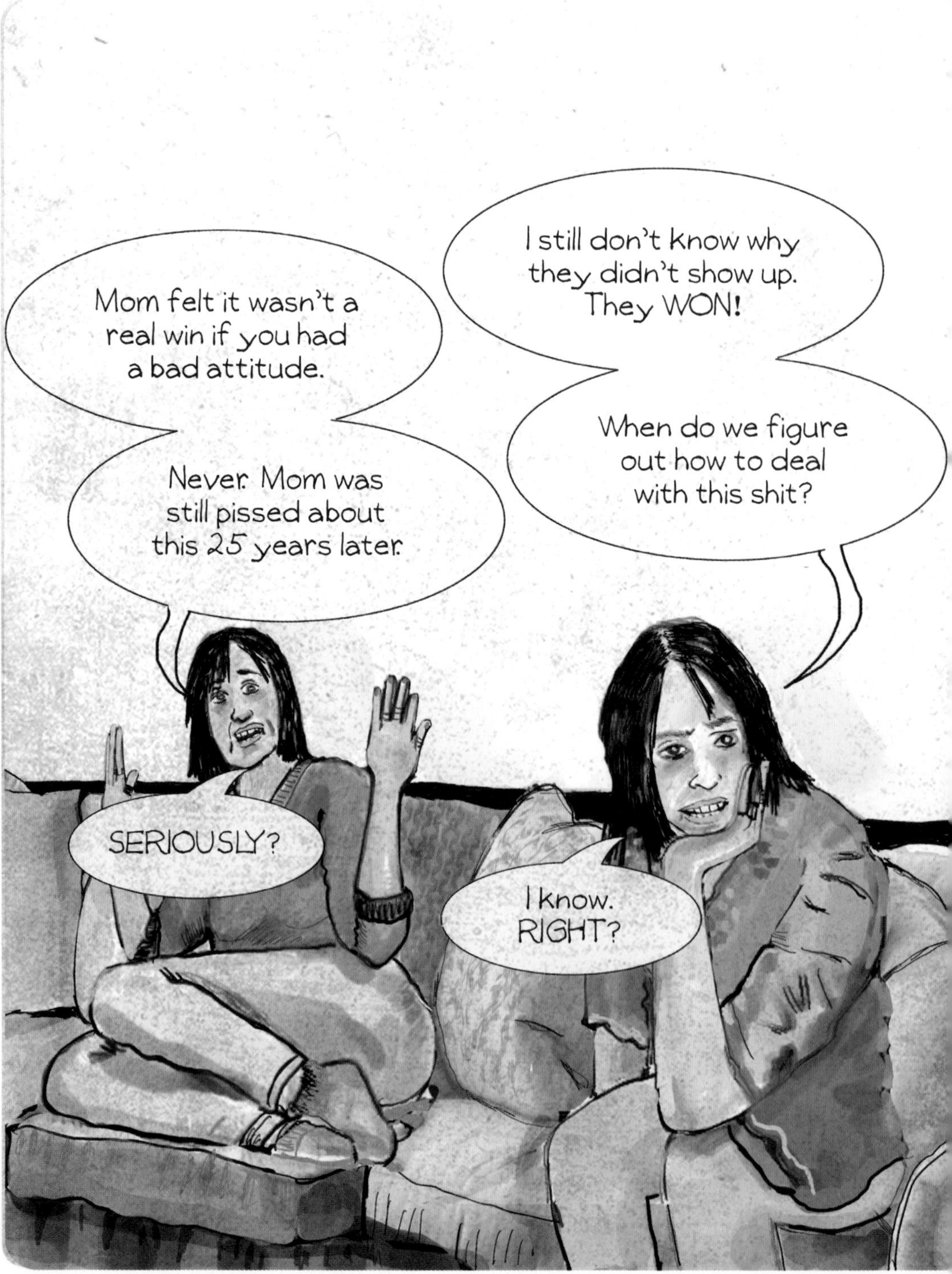
Mom felt it wasn't a real win if you had a bad attitude.
Never. Mom was still pissed about this 25 years later.
I still don't know why they didn't show up. They WON!
When do we figure out how to deal with this shit?
SERIOUSLY?
I know. RIGHT?

By now, my parents and I were so sick of each other that there were no tears shed when they dropped me off at UC Berkeley . . . where, by the way, the in-state tuition fee that year was seventy-five dollars a quarter.

I was already enough of a comedy geek to have made my way, alone, into San Francisco to attend what I now know was one of Lenny Bruce's last performances. Hoping to hear obscenities, I had no idea how to process the ironic but not very funny real court transcripts depicting his relentless pursuit by the government that he stood on stage and read.

And Officer Ryan is standing there listening to the show as the defendant comes out, sits down in a chair and begins a monologue, telling stories about his activities in show business. And he starts talking with, we believe, his agent. And either HE says, or THE AGENT says, that he is NOT going to book him "because there's too many COCKSUCKERS." THIS is the defendant's statement in a PUBLIC PLACE on October 4, 1961.

Ho hum.

THE MOTHERS

> Berkeley was a place where it was mostly
> okay to be funny. That was a relief. A big relief.

THURSDAY, SEPTEMBER 1, 1966

The hamburgers for lunch weren't too bad. But when they served the exact same ones for dinner, Carol and I took ours back to the room and, along with some parsley and a few lemon rinds, made a mobile to hang from the dorm room ceiling.

I was so much happier living away from home that I began making a serious effort to get along with my mother.

An important thing to be learned is that it is essential to maintain your calm at all times. I am learning how to deal with my furious explosive mother. Whenever she wants something, she requests it by screaming at full volume, a howling temper tantrum, hurling questions at me that can't be answered. Then demanding an answer anyway. But I figured out just to take a deep breath and say nothing. Of course, that makes her even madder because I'm not reacting. And I don't know what to do about that. But still...

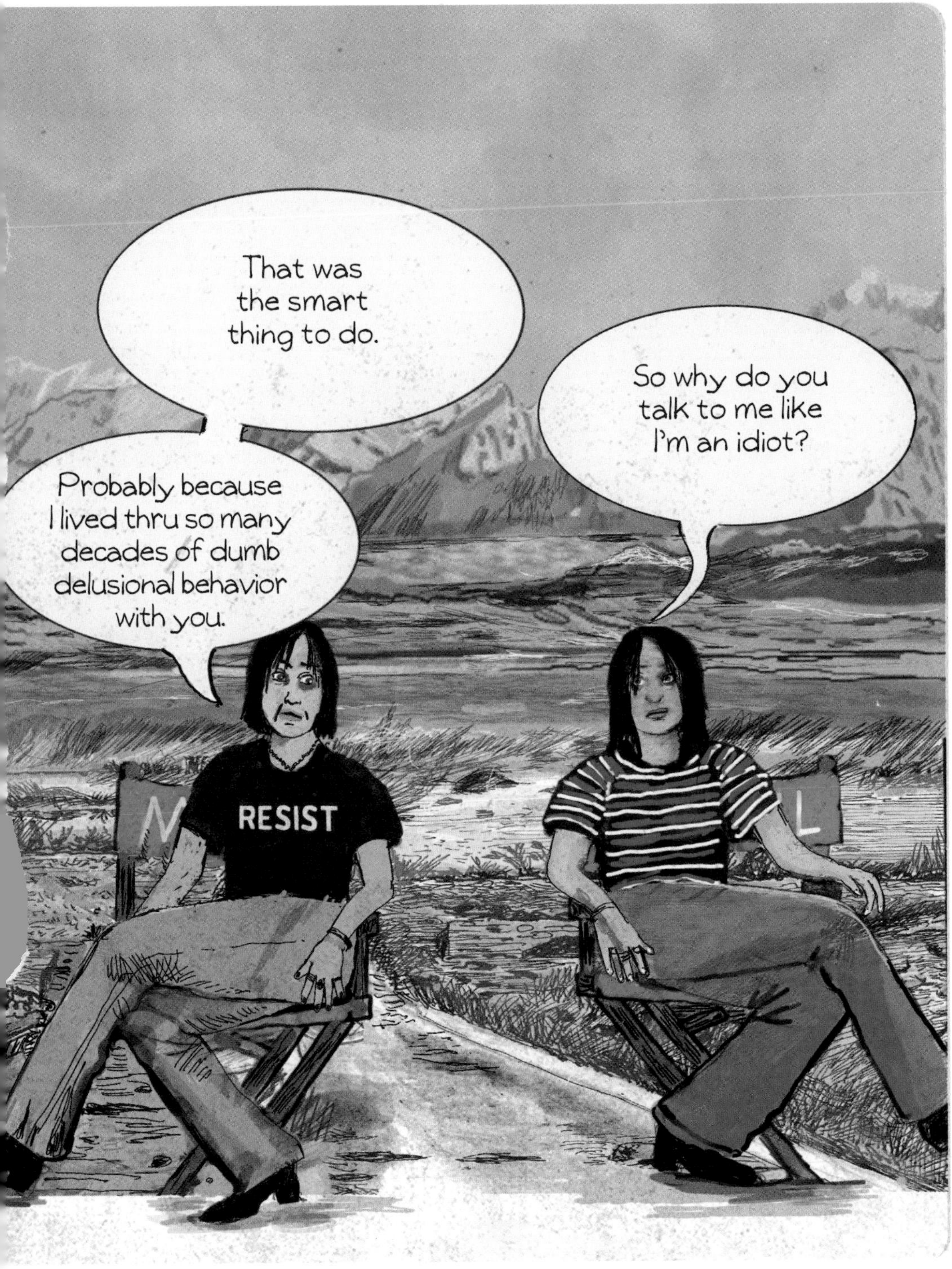
That was the smart thing to do.
So why do you talk to me like I'm an idiot?
Probably because I lived thru so many decades of dumb delusional behavior with you.
RESIST
M
L

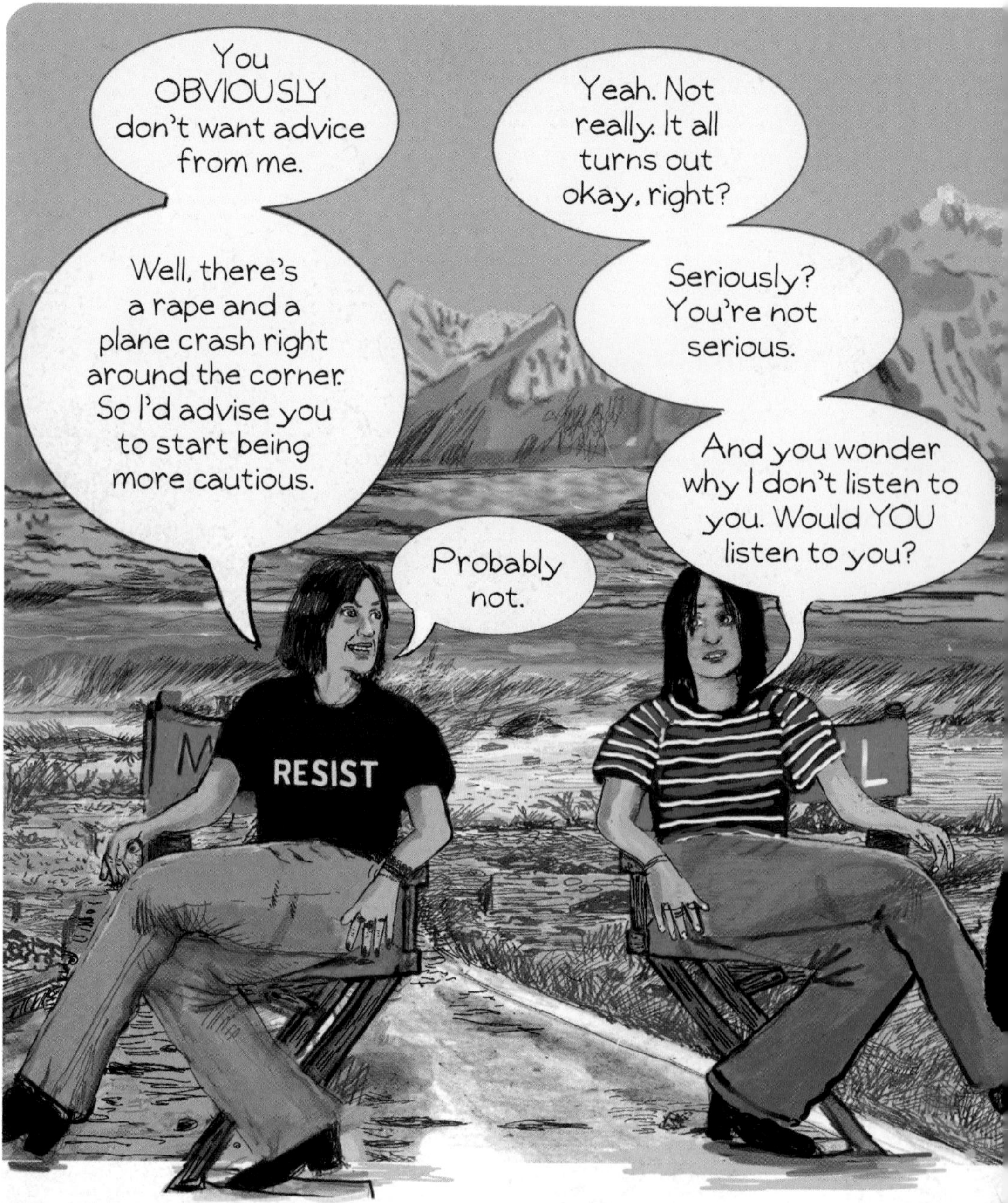
You OBVIOUSLY don't want advice from me.
Yeah. Not really. It all turns out okay, right?
Well, there's a rape and a plane crash right around the corner. So I'd advise you to start being more cautious.
Seriously? You're not serious.
Probably not.
And you wonder why I don't listen to you. Would YOU listen to you?
RESIST

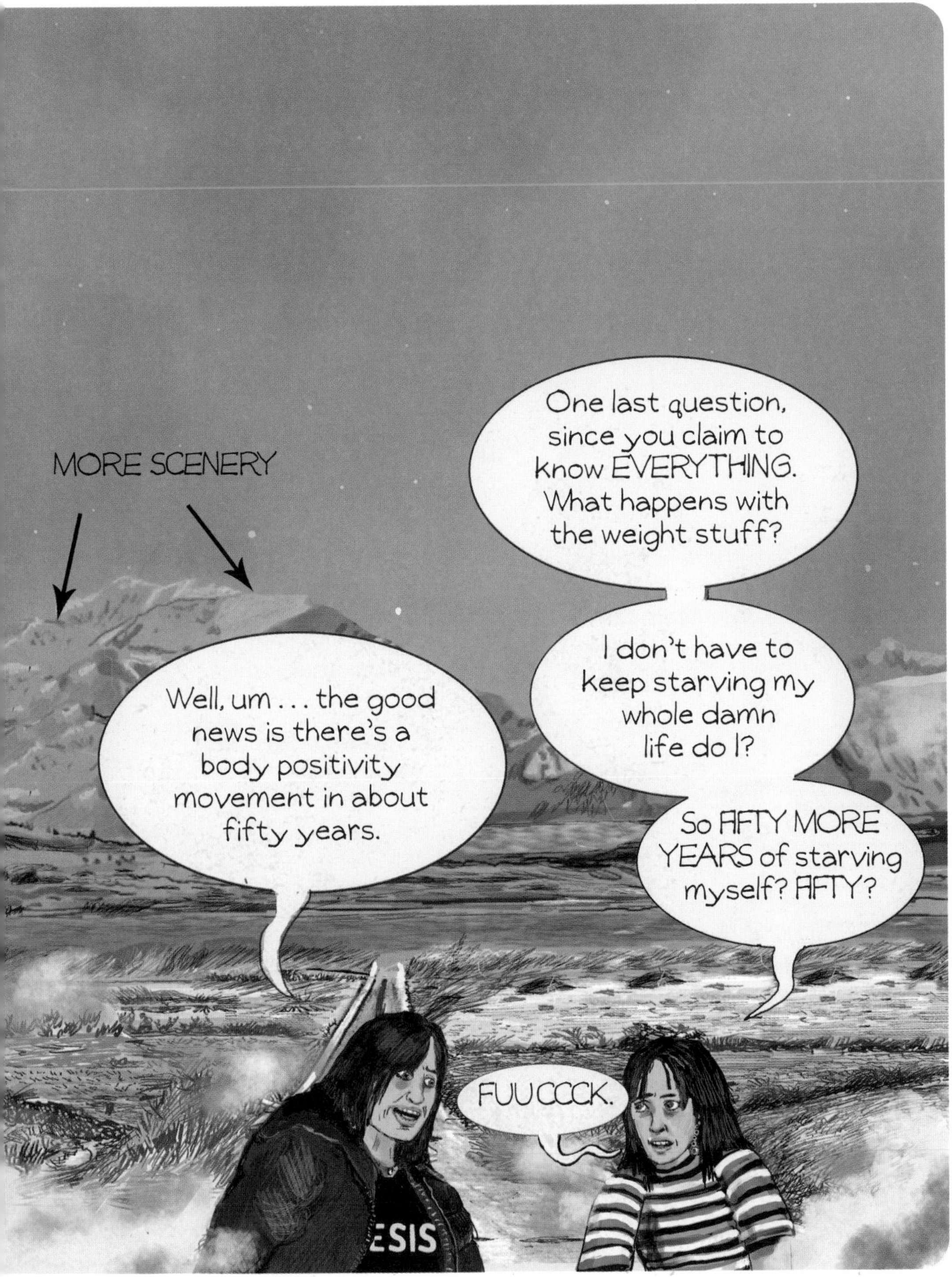
MORE SCENERY
One last question, since you claim to know EVERYTHING. What happens with the weight stuff?
I don't have to keep starving my whole damn life do I?
So FIFTY MORE YEARS of starving myself? FIFTY?
Well, um . . . the good news is there's a body positivity movement in about fifty years.
FUUCCCK.
ESIS

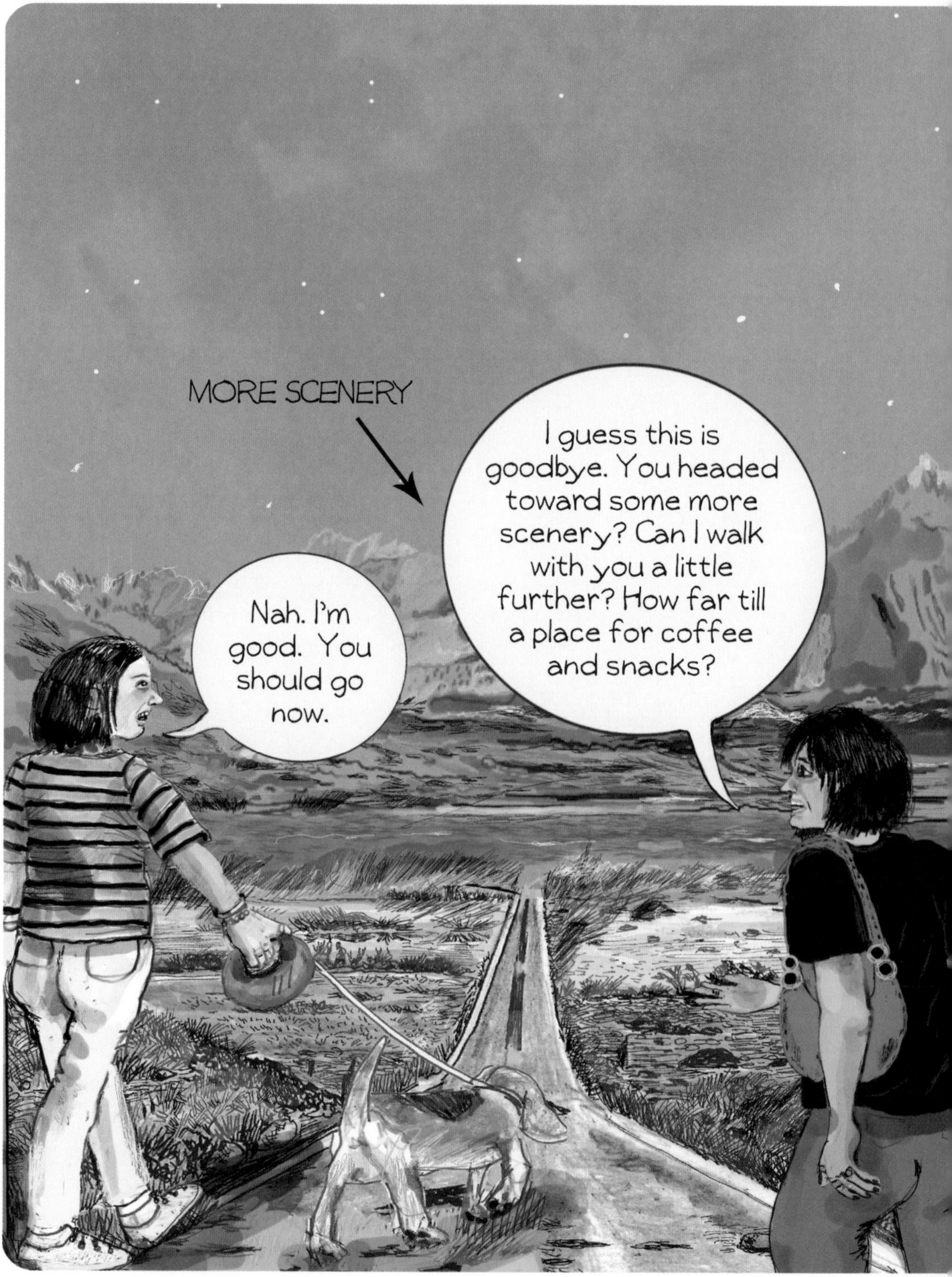
MORE SCENERY
Nah. I'm good. You should go now.
I guess this is goodbye. You headed toward some more scenery? Can I walk with you a little further? How far till a place for coffee and snacks?

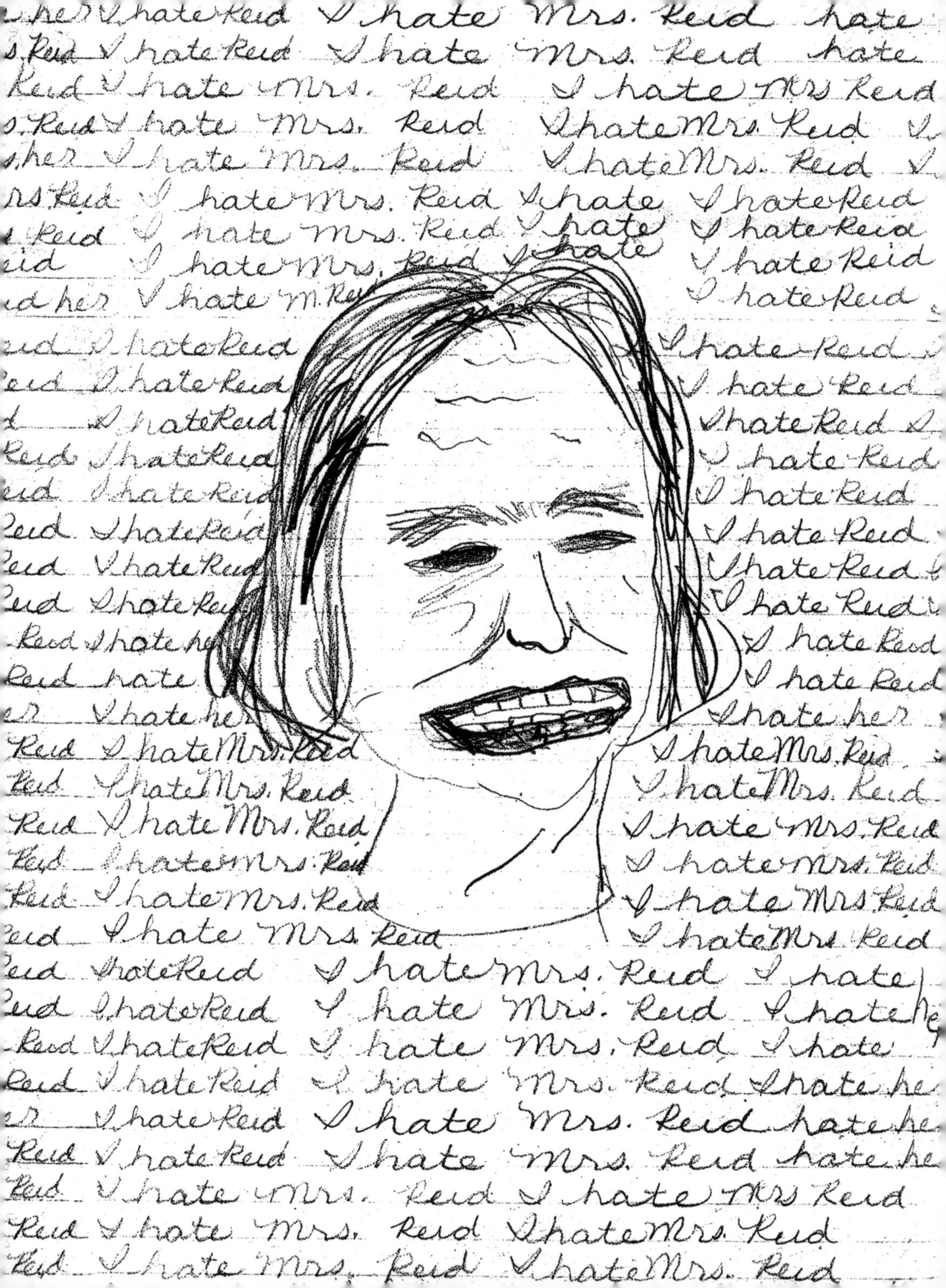
her I hate Reid I hate Mrs. Reid hate
s Reid I hate Reid I hate Mrs. Reid hate
Reid I hate Mrs. Reid I hate Mrs Reid
s. Reid I hate Mrs. Reid I hate Mrs. Reid I
s. her I hate Mrs. Reid I hate Mrs. Reid I
rs Reid I hate Mrs. Reid I hate I hate Reid
Reid I hate Mrs. Reid I hate I hate Reid
id I hate Mrs. Reid I hate I hate Reid
d her I hate M. Reid I hate Reid
id I hate Reid I hate Reid
Reid I hate Reid I hate Reid
I hate Reid I hate Reid
Reid I hate Reid I hate Reid
id I hate Reid I hate Reid
Reid I hate Reid I hate Reid
Reid I hate Reid I hate Reid
Reid I hate Reid I hate Reid
Reid I hate her I hate Reid
Reid hate I hate Reid
er I hate her I hate her
Reid I hate Mrs. Reid I hate Mrs. Reid
Reid I hate Mrs. Reid I hate Mrs. Reid
Reid I hate Mrs. Reid I hate Mrs. Reid
Reid I hate Mrs. Reid I hate Mrs. Reid
Reid I hate Mrs. Reid I hate Mrs. Reid
Reid I hate Mrs. Reid I hate Mrs. Reid
Reid I hate Reid I hate Mrs. Reid I hate
Reid I hate Reid I hate Mrs. Reid I hate her
Reid I hate Reid I hate Mrs. Reid I hate
Reid I hate Reid I hate Mrs. Reid I hate her
er I hate Reid I hate Mrs. Reid hate her
Reid I hate Reid I hate Mrs. Reid hate her
Reid I hate Mrs. Reid I hate Mrs Reid
Reid I hate Mrs. Reid I hate Mrs. Reid
Reid I hate Mrs. Reid I hate Mrs. Reid